AF422254

Fintech: Redefining Financial Services

Innovations, Challenges, and Opportunities in the Digital Era

Sophia Reynolds

© Copyright 2024 - All rights reserved.

The content contained within this book may not be reproduced, duplicated or transmitted without direct written permission from the author or the publisher.

Under no circumstances will any blame or legal responsibility be held against the publisher, or author, for any damages, reparation, or monetary loss due to the information contained within this book, either directly or indirectly.

Legal Notice:

This book is copyright protected. It is only for personal use. You cannot amend, distribute, sell, use, quote or paraphrase any part, or the content within this book, without the consent of the author or publisher.

Disclaimer Notice:

Please note the information contained within this document is for educational and entertainment purposes only. All effort has been executed to present accurate, up to date, reliable, complete information. No warranties of any kind are declared or implied. Readers acknowledge that the author is not engaging in the rendering of legal, financial, medical or professional advice. The content within this book has been derived from various sources. Please consult a licensed professional before attempting any techniques outlined in this book.

By reading this document, the reader agrees that under no circumstances is the author responsible for any losses, direct or indirect, that are incurred as a result of the use of information contained within this document, including, but not limited to, errors, omissions, or inaccuracies.

Table of Contents

INTRODUCTION

"Fintech: Redefining Financial Services: Innovations, Challenges, and Opportunities in the Digital Era," a conscientious examination of how financial technology can revolutionize the financial industry. The financial services industry is leading this transition in an era where electronic innovation transforms every aspect of our lives. Fintech, the merging of finance and technology, is causing previously unheard-of shifts in everything from loan applications and asset insurance to payment methods and investment management.

This book delves into the intricate world of Fintech, unveiling the revolutionary creations that are reshaping traditional financial services. We'll explore the advent of digital payments, the evolution of cryptocurrencies and blockchain technology, and the ascent of robo-advisors in wealth management. Each innovation is not just a technological marvel, but a practical solution that enhances accessibility, user experiences, and financial operations.

However, with innovation comes challenges. This book addresses the crucial issues of cybersecurity, regulatory compliance, and the technological hurdles that Fintech organizations must navigate. It is imperative for all stakeholders in this dynamic sector to grasp these complexities, as they are integral to the future of Fintech.

We will also examine Fintech's many opportunities, including promoting financial inclusion, customizing financial services, and developing strategic alliances. This book provides significant insights into the current and prospective state of the Fintech industry through empirical case studies and prospective analysis.

CHAPTER I

The Evolution of Financial Technology

Historical background of financial services

The financial services industry's history is a testament to human resourcefulness and the relentless pursuit of more efficient ways to transfer, manage, and grow wealth. Financial technology, or Fintech, has evolved from the early days of bartering products and services to the intricate digital financial systems of today. This evolution underscores the dynamic interplay between innovation, regulation, and economic development, showcasing the industry's remarkable resilience.

Historically, barter systems were used for trade and commerce, allowing for directly exchanging products and services without needing money. The requirement for a double coincidence of wants—for each party to a transaction to have the precise commodities or services that the other desires—limited this system from the start. The invention of money—first as commodities like precious metals and shells and then as coinage—revolutionized trade by offering a dependable store of value and a common medium of exchange. The foundation for increasingly intricate financial organizations and systems was created by this breakthrough.

An important turning point in the history of financial services was the founding of banks. Ancient Mesopotamia and the Roman Empire saw the establishment of the first banks, frequently used as lending and safe deposit locations by temples. Italy experienced a surge in merchant banking during the Middle Ages, with Medici families among the most influential in providing funds for European trade. These pioneer banks supplied letters of credit and bills of exchange, which made long-distance trading easier and lowered the dangers involved in moving significant quantities of cash.

More advanced financial tools and institutions were introduced during the economic revolutions of the 17th and 18th centuries. Bank of England, in 1694, central banks gave governments the ability to control national debt and print money. The founding of the Amsterdam Stock Exchange by the Dutch East India Company in 1602 made the stock markets essential venues for capital raising. These changes promoted economic expansion and established the framework for contemporary financial markets.

The Industrial Revolution further expedited the development of financial services in the 19th century. Investment banking emerged as a response to the demand for large-scale funding for infrastructure projects, including factories and railroads. The era saw the introduction of limited liability for corporations and the growth of insurance services as financial advancements. Financial transactions became quicker and more effective due to the communication revolution brought about by the telegraph and, later, the telephone.

The 20th century saw the advent of digital financial services and the development of electronic banking. The 1950s and 1960s saw the introduction of computers, which allowed banks to automate procedures and enhance record-keeping. Diners Club and American

Express spearheaded the 1950s credit card revolution, fundamentally altering consumer spending patterns and establishing the foundation for modern digital payment systems. The 1973 establishment of the Society for Worldwide Interbank Financial Telecommunication (SWIFT), which standardized cross-border financial transactions, enhanced trade and investment worldwide.

A new era in financial technology began with the development of the Internet in the late 20th century. Online banking became popular in the 1990s, providing customers unmatched access to their accounts and financial services. Online stock trading platforms increased during the dot-com boom, democratizing access to financial markets. E-commerce behemoths like PayPal transformed online payment systems, helping to develop widely used digital wallets and payment apps.

Fintech technologies have exploded in the twenty-first century, propelled by blockchain, AI, and mobile technology developments. Thanks to mobile banking and payment apps, financial services are now easier to obtain, especially in developing nations with weak traditional banking infrastructure. By employing algorithms to offer individualized financial advice, robo-advisors are expanding the reach of wealth management services to a broader demographic. Providing decentralized and transparent alternatives to established banking systems, cryptocurrencies, and blockchain technology are upending preconceived conceptions about money and financial transactions.

While the pace of innovation in financial technology is rapid, there have been challenges in its development. Concerns regarding security, privacy, and systemic risk have arisen due to regulatory frameworks' incapacity to keep up with technological breakthroughs. As financial services have transitioned online, cybersecurity threats have significantly increased, necessitating the implementation of robust safeguards to protect sensitive data and maintain customer trust. However, these challenges are manageable. The potential of Fintech to overcome these hurdles and continue to revolutionize the financial services industry is a source of optimism.

In summary, the development of financial technology is a tale of ongoing invention and adaptation. Every development, from the earliest days of barter and money to the modern digital and decentralized systems, has been built upon the foundations created by earlier generations. Fintech's prospects and challenges will continue influencing financial services, promoting global financial resource accessibility and stimulating economic growth. Financial technology is still in its early stages of development, and the next few years should bring forth even more revolutionary developments.

The rise of digital technology

Due to the rise of digital technology, almost every element of modern life has undergone a fundamental transformation, including how we work, communicate, and manage our finances. This vast technological transformation has created a highly linked and dynamic world typified by the quick creation and spread of digital gadgets, the Internet, and numerous software applications. The path of digital technology, characterized by constant invention and adaptation, has profoundly changed industries and communities, improving ease and efficiency.

The mid-20th century saw the development of early computers and the advent of the transistor, which set the groundwork for the digital age. The 1947 invention of the transistor transformed electronics by making it possible to build more compact, dependable, and efficient devices. This discovery made it possible to construct integrated circuits, which reduced the size of electronic components and allowed for the development of the first microprocessors in the 1950s and 1960s. The age of personal computers (PCs) began in the 1970s with the introduction of microprocessors, which allowed small businesses and people to access computing power for the first time.

Digital technology was introduced into homes and offices worldwide during the personal computer revolution of the 1980s and 1990s. Businesses like Apple, Microsoft, and IBM were essential in popularizing PCs, producing intuitive software, and fostering a competitive environment that accelerated the development of new hardware and software. Adoption was further accelerated by the emergence of graphical user interfaces (GUIs), such as those included in Microsoft Windows and Apple Macintosh operating systems, which made computers more approachable for non-technical people.

The Internet's growth coincided with the popularity of personal computers, turning digital technology into a worldwide phenomenon. With the development of the World Wide Web in the 1990s, the Internet—first imagined as a military and academic research network in the 1960s—transformed into a commercial and public arena. Tim Berners-Lee's 1989 creation of the web established a standardized method for accessing and sharing information via the Internet using web browsers and hypertext links. This invention made information more accessible and paved the way for social media, e-commerce, and other online services.

The internet rumble of the late 1990s and early 2000s was characterized by the rapid growth of online services and the emergence of dot-com enterprises. Search engines like Google revolutionized how we locate and access information, while e-commerce behemoths like Amazon and eBay revolutionized retail. Social media platforms have reshaped people's communication and engagement, bringing new forms of social connectivity and community. Friendster and Myspace were the first, followed by Facebook, Twitter, and Instagram.

The emergence of digital technology was further expedited in the 21st century with the introduction of mobile technology. With the release of smartphones, first the BlackBerry and then the Apple iPhone in 2007, we could carry sophisticated computers. Smartphones provided previously unheard-of levels of ease and mobility by combining the capabilities of a laptop, camera, and communication device. The emergence of mobile applications has revolutionized various sectors by offering inventive solutions for tasks such as travel (Uber, Lyft), accommodation (Airbnb), personal finance (Venmo, PayPal), and entertainment (Netflix, Spotify).

The exposure to digital technology has significantly impacted the nature of work and the workplace. By removing geographical obstacles and facilitating remote work and worldwide cooperation, the Internet and digital communication tools have made the workforce more adaptable and dynamic. Cloud computing has further improved corporate efficiency and scalability by enabling the processing and storing of data on remote computers. Automation technology and digital platforms have streamlined operations, cut costs and raising production in several industries.

Digital technology has revolutionized established industries and spawned whole new markets and business models. The gig economy has become a significant job sector, defined by short-term and freelance labor arrangements made possible by digital networks. Worker rights and job security are among the issues that come with the new prospects for flexibility and revenue generation brought forth by companies like TaskRabbit, Upwork, and Uber.

The development of digital technology has brought forth several issues and worries in addition to its many advantages. As more private and sensitive data is exchanged and stored online, privacy, security, and data protection concerns are becoming more and more critical. Threats to cybersecurity, such as phishing, ransomware, and hacking, put people and businesses in danger. Furthermore, the gap between people who have access to digital technologies and those who do not is still known as the "digital divide," it has the potential to exacerbate social and economic inequality.

The speed at which technology is developing also raises concerns about the future of labor and the economy. Certain jobs may become obsolete due to automation and artificial intelligence (AI), requiring workers to adapt and retrain. These technologies, however, also have the potential to spur innovation, raise living standards generally, and generate new businesses and jobs.

In summary, digital technology's development has fundamentally changed how we work, live, and engage with the outside world. Digital technology has fueled previously unheard-of advancement and connectedness, from the early days of transistors and mainframe computers to smartphones, cloud computing, and artificial intelligence. The path has been challenging, but as digital technology advances, new opportunities and innovations are expected to arise, creating a more dynamic, efficient, and linked future than in the past.

Key milestones in Fintech development

Several significant turning points in the development of financial technology, or Fintech, have drastically changed the financial services industry. Every milestone, from the launch of the first electronic banking systems to the emergence of cryptocurrencies and blockchain technology, signifies a significant advancement in the provision, accessibility, and use of financial services.

Credit cards were introduced in the 1950s, marking one of the first significant turning points in the history of Fintech. The introduction of the Diners Club card in 1950 and the American Express card in 1958 transformed consumer spending by providing a practical and safe way to make cashless purchases. Credit cards revolutionized the consumer finance scene by offering a convenient substitute for cash and checks and paved the way for later digital payment methods.

The introduction of automated teller machines (ATMs) in the 1960s revolutionized banking by giving consumers round-the-clock access to their money. When Barclays Bank opened its first ATM in London in 1967, users could withdraw cash and carry out simple banking operations without the assistance of a human teller. This breakthrough made more advanced digital banking solutions possible, improving the efficiency and convenience of financial services.

The development of electronic funds transfer (EFT) systems in the 1970s was another significant turning point. EFT systems allow money to be transferred electronically between bank accounts, making transactions faster and more effective. By giving banks access to a safe and dependable communication network, the Society for Worldwide Interbank Financial Telecommunication (SWIFT) was founded in 1973, standardizing international financial transactions and promoting trade and investment on a global scale.

The emergence of online banking in the 1980s and 1990s brought about even more changes to the financial services sector. Thanks to the development of personal computers and the Internet, bank customers can now manage their accounts, transfer money, and pay bills online from their homes. Online trading platforms also existed at this time, democratizing access to financial markets and making it possible for anybody to purchase and sell equities with previously unheard-of simplicity.

E-commerce took off in the late 1990s and early 2000s thanks to the expansion of the Internet and the creation of safe online payment methods. By offering a secure environment for online transactions, businesses like PayPal, which was established in 1998, have transformed the online payment industry. The success of PayPal established the foundation for creating digital wallets and mobile payment solutions while showcasing the possibilities of digital payment systems.

Another significant turning point in the growth of Fintech occurred with the emergence of smartphones in the late 2000s. The introduction of the Apple iPhone in 2007 and the popularity of mobile applications revolutionized how consumers used financial services. Customers could use mobile banking apps on their cellphones to check account balances, transfer funds, and deposit checks, among other banking functions. Mobile banking gained popularity quickly due to its accessibility and ease, especially in areas with poor access to traditional financial infrastructure.

The emergence of mobile payment platforms like Google Wallet and Apple Pay significantly transformed the Fintech industry. With the help of these digital wallets, customers could use their cell phones to make payments, providing a safe and practical substitute for conventional payment methods. Peer-to-peer (P2P) payment services like Venmo and Square Cash, which enable instantaneous money transfers between individuals, have since been added to the list of mobile payment alternatives.

The late 2000s saw the rise of cryptocurrencies and blockchain technology, considered one of the most significant turning points in the Fintech industry. The first decentralized cryptocurrency, Bitcoin, was unveiled in

2009 by an unidentified individual or group named Satoshi Nakamoto. It provided a novel means of conducting transactions without using intermediaries like banks. Since then, numerous facets of financial services have benefited from applying the underlying blockchain technology, a decentralized ledger that tracks transactions over a network of computers. These applications range from safe and transparent record-keeping to intelligent contracts and decentralized finance (DeFi) platforms.

Another critical turning point in the Fintech space was the development of robo-advisors in the 2010s. Robo-advisors automate, providing individualized financial advice and portfolio management through artificial intelligence and algorithms. Thanks to the innovation of firms like Wealth front and Betterment, financial services are now more widely available and reasonably priced. The emergence of robo-advisors is a prime example of how artificial intelligence and machine learning have the potential to transform wealth management and financial planning completely.

Fintech development has advanced further in recent years with the revolt of application programming interfaces (APIs) and open banking. Open banking programs have encouraged more competition and innovation in the financial services sector by requiring banks to share client data with third-party providers (with the consumer's approval). APIs make it possible for various financial services and systems to integrate seamlessly, which speeds up the creation of new Fintech products and improves the user experience overall.

Fintech adoption has also been accelerated by the COVID-19 epidemic, which has sped up the transition to digital financial services. Fintech solutions are used more frequently due to the demands of online financial management, remote banking, and contactless payment systems. Digital banking, mobile payments, and online investment platforms have all grown significantly during this time, demonstrating the Fintech industry's adaptability and resilience.

To sum up, the evolution of Fintech has been marked by several significant turning points that have gradually changed the financial services industry. Each major development in the industry, from the creation of credit cards and ATMs to the emergence of blockchain technology and robo-advisors, has enhanced the availability and delivery of financial services. As Fintech develops further, it is expected to deliver more innovations that will impact the future of finance by improving accessibility, efficiency, and security for both individuals and enterprises.

CHAPTER II

Digital Payments and Money Transfers

Mobile wallets and digital payments

The advent of electronic payments and money transfers, particularly through mobile wallets, has ushered in a new era in financial transactions. This transformation is a testament to the ongoing evolution of technology and its profound impact on the financial industry. Digital payments and mobile wallets are not just tools, but catalysts that reshape consumer behavior and business operations, offering unparalleled convenience, security, and efficiency.

Smartphone applications, known as mobile wallets, also called digital wallets, allow users to conduct transactions without actual cards or cash by securely storing payment information. The development of near-field communication (NFC) technology and the widespread use of smartphones in the late 2000s helped popularize the idea. Early innovators like Apple Pay, Samsung Pay, and Google Wallet (now Google Pay) paved the way for broader adoption by providing a simple and easy way to pay for goods and services.

One of the key benefits of mobile wallets is the empowerment they offer. By linking credit or debit cards to a mobile wallet, users can make payments with a single tap or scan, eliminating the need to carry cash or multiple cards. Mobile wallets are designed to enhance the user experience, incorporating features such as budgeting tools, loyalty programs, and transaction history. This integration allows users to access exclusive deals from retailers and track their spending in real-time, enabling them to manage their money more effectively and feel in control of their financial decisions.

Another critical component of digital payments and mobile wallets is security. Cash and physical credit cards are examples of traditional payment methods that are susceptible to fraud and theft. Mobile wallets, on the other hand, use cutting-edge security technologies to safeguard user data. Sensitive payment information is kept safe during transactions thanks to features like tokenization, encryption, and biometric authentication (facial recognition and fingerprints). Tokenization lowers the possibility of data breaches by substituting a distinct digital token for credit card information. By adding a layer of security, biometric authentication makes it more difficult for unauthorized users to access the wallet.

The increasing popularity of mobile wallets has enabled the proliferation of peer-to-peer (P2P) payment platforms. Users can now quickly and easily transfer money to friends and family using services like Venmo, PayPal, and Cash App, which are becoming widely used. These platforms allow for easy transfers between bank accounts or within the app itself by integrating with mobile wallets. The social component of peer-to-peer payment platforms, which will enable users to add emoticons and messages to transactions, has enhanced the intimacy and engagement of money transfers. P2P payments are famous for speed and ease, especially with younger audiences.

Digital payments have also revolutionized business operations. E-commerce has grown exponentially, partly due to the security and convenience of online payment options. Online merchants can increase their customer base and reach by accepting payments from people worldwide. Integrating with e-commerce platforms, mobile wallets lower cart abandonment rates and enable one-click checkouts. Digital payments also facilitate subscription and recurring billing models, giving companies a consistent source of income.

The COVID-19 pandemic hastened the uptake of mobile wallets and electronic payments. Lockdowns and social distancing policies prompted businesses and consumers to seek contactless payment options to reduce face-to-face interactions. Paying with a smartphone tap has made mobile wallets a desirable option. Digital payments are becoming more widely accepted because many companies that had previously only accepted cash or credit cards quickly adapted to receive them. The pandemic highlighted the value of adaptable and durable payment systems, emphasizing digital payments' role in providing convenience and continuity in trying times.

Despite their many advantages, the emergence of digital payments and mobile wallets comes with challenges. The digital divide, which refers to unequal access to digital payment options among various geographic and demographic groups, is one of the main issues. Mobile wallet adoption may be slower in developing nations, where smartphone adoption and internet access may be less familiar. To close this gap and guarantee that everyone can benefit from digital payments, initiatives to advance financial inclusion and upgrade digital infrastructure are essential.

Regulations must also be considered. As the use of digital payments increases, regulators need to ensure that these platforms run openly and securely. Regulators also need to focus on important issues like consumer protection, data privacy, and anti-money laundering (AML) compliance. Innovation and regulation must be balanced to promote a secure and long-lasting digital payments ecosystem.

In conclusion, digital payments and mobile wallets have not only revolutionized our financial landscape but also hold the promise of a more inclusive future. They have been embraced by consumers and businesses alike, thanks to their simplicity, security, and efficiency. As technology continues to advance, these tools will likely become even more integrated into our daily lives, offering new features and functionalities that enhance the user experience. However, to ensure that the benefits of digital payments are universally accessible and to foster a more resilient and inclusive financial system, it is crucial to address issues of regulation and accessibility.

Peer-to-peer (P2P) payment platforms

Peer-to-peer (P2P) payment systems are revolutionizing how people send money to one another and have become a powerful force in the financial industry. By avoiding traditional banking channels, these platforms use the power of digital technology to enable quick, safe, and convenient money transfers. The emergence of peer-to-peer payment platforms, like Venmo, PayPal, and Cash App, indicates broader patterns toward digital transformation and the growing need for smooth financial services.

With the introduction of e-commerce and the Internet in the late 1990s and early 2000s, P2P payment platforms came into being. Founded in 1998, PayPal was one of the first companies in this field, helping eBay and other auction sites with online payments. It made it possible for people to send and receive money using their email addresses, eliminating the need for intricate bank transactions. The tremendous success of PayPal's business model paved the way for creating additional P2P payment options.

Convenience is a significant factor in P2P payment platform adoption. Conventional means of transferring funds, like bank transfers and check writing, frequently entail drawn-out procedures and costs. P2P platforms simplify this process by enabling instantaneous fund transfers with a few smartphone taps. Users can quickly and easily transfer money between P2P accounts by linking their bank accounts or credit/debit cards to them. The younger generation, who are used to the speed and efficiency of digital services, finds this ease of use especially appealing.

An additional noteworthy benefit of peer-to-peer payment platforms is security. To safeguard users' financial data and transactions, these systems use cutting-edge encryption and authentication technologies. Features like secure sockets layer (SSL) encryption, biometric verification (facial recognition or fingerprint), and two-factor authentication protect the data from cyber threats and unauthorized access. Furthermore, most P2P platforms provide fraud prevention tools, allowing users to feel secure about the security of their transactions.

P2P payment systems improve the user experience by adding social components. For example, the 2009-launched Venmo gained popularity due to its social feed feature and functionality. In an interface reminiscent of social media, users can add emojis and comments, view other people's transactions, and share their payment activities with friends. Financial transactions become more engaging and enjoyable with the addition of this social component, which adds a layer of interaction. Additionally, it encourages openness and a sense of community among users.

P2P payment platforms have significantly changed many facets of personal finance and business operations. Without using cash or checks, these platforms provide individuals an easy way to divide bills, share expenses, and send money to friends and family. This is especially helpful when timely and precise money transfers are necessary, such as group dinners, shared housing costs, and travel expenses. Transmitting and receiving money instantaneously improves financial management and lessens the inconvenience of using conventional payment methods.

P2P payment platforms have given businesses, tiny and medium-sized enterprises (SMEs), additional benefits. Unlike traditional payment processors, these systems allow companies to take payments directly from customers with minimal setup or transaction fees. Small business owners, gig economy employees, and freelancers who require flexible and affordable payment options will particularly benefit from this. Furthermore, the checkout process has been streamlined by incorporating P2P payment options into mobile apps and e-commerce platforms, increasing customer satisfaction and driving sales.

However,, several issues and concerns remain to consider as P2P payment platforms continue to increase. Regulatory compliance is one of the main issues. These platforms must abide by anti-money laundering (AML) laws and other financial compliance requirements since they enable the transfer of funds. Platform suppliers must strike a careful balance between upholding user security and privacy and following these laws. P2P platforms will probably come under more regulatory scrutiny as they grow and become more integrated with larger financial systems.

Ensuring accessibility and inclusivity presents another difficulty. The adoption of P2P payment platforms in developing nations may be constrained by technological and infrastructural obstacles, even though these platforms are extensively utilized in developed regions with high smartphone penetration and internet access. Achieving inclusive financial services requires initiatives to advance digital literacy, enhance internet accessibility, and open up these platforms to a broader user base.

P2P payment platform competition is likewise changing quickly. The market constantly changes due to innovations and entrants providing better user experiences, cheaper prices, and more features. Platforms are adding features like investing, budgeting tools, and even cryptocurrency transactions beyond basic money transfers. This diversification aims to build extensive financial ecosystems that meet the needs of a broad spectrum of users.

In conclusion, peer-to-peer (P2P) payment platforms provide unmatched ease, security, and social interaction and have entirely transformed how money is transferred between people and enterprises. They have significantly impacted business operations and personal finance, simplified transactions and promoting a culture of instantaneous, digital payments. To ensure sustainable and inclusive financial innovation, these platforms must address regulatory, inclusivity, and competitive challenges as they expand. P2P payments are expected to continue to progress and integrate, advancing the development of the digital financial environment.

Innovations in remittances and cross-border transfers

The remittance sector, which includes money sent by migrants to their friends and family back home, has long been an important part of the world economy. Remittances were previously made possible by conventional channels like wire transfers, money transfer operators (MTOs), and banks. These channels were frequently associated with excessive costs, protracted processing times, and restricted accessibility. However, the emergence of digital technology and creative financial solutions has changed the remittance scene, opening new channels, cutting expenses, and boosting effectiveness.

The advent of digital remittance platforms and mobile money services is one of the biggest innovations in remittances. These platforms have not only revolutionized the process but also brought a host of benefits for migrants and their families. They provide quick, safe, and affordable money transfer options by utilizing digital infrastructure and mobile technology. Remittance companies such as TransferWise, WorldRemit, and Remitly have caused a stir in the market by offering competitive exchange rates, clear pricing, and easy-to-use interfaces. There is no longer a need for users to physically visit brick and mortar establishments because transfers can be started online or through mobile apps. This ease of use is especially beneficial for immigrants who might be employed in isolated or underprivileged regions.

Blockchain technology has revolutionized cross-border transfers and remittances as well. Without intermediaries, secure and transparent transactions are made possible by blockchain, a decentralized and unchangeable ledger. Because it enables real-time cross-border transfers at a fraction of the cost of conventional methods, Ripple, a blockchain-based payment protocol, has gained traction in the remittance industry. Banks and payment providers can settle transactions instantly thanks to Ripple's financial institution network or RippleNet, passing the costly and time-consuming correspondent banking system. Cross-border payments could be revolutionized, becoming more affordable, quicker, and accessible to underprivileged groups.

Integrating digital wallets with cryptocurrencies is another cutting-edge method of sending money back home. Users can send and receive money internationally using cryptocurrencies like Bitcoin and Ethereum through platforms like Abra and Coins. Ph. This lowers costs and transaction times by allowing migrants to avoid conventional banking systems and remittance channels. Cryptocurrencies have several benefits for cross-border transfers, such as minimal transaction fees, global accessibility, and improved security. However, issues with volatility, regulatory compliance, and adoption barriers still need to be resolved for adoption to be widely adopted.

Additionally, the growth of mobile money services in developing nations has made cross-border transfers and remittances easier. Even without a traditional bank account, users can store and transfer money using mobile phones thanks to mobile money platforms like GCash in the Philippines and M-Pesa in Kenya. Due to the ease with which these services enable people to send and receive money domestically and internationally, they have grown in popularity among the unbanked and underbanked population. The reach and usefulness of these platforms are further increased by mobile money interoperability agreements between various providers, which facilitate smooth cross-border transactions.

Innovations in Know Your Customer (KYC) procedures and identity verification have improved the efficiency and security of remittances. By enabling secure user authentication and onboarding, biometric authentication technologies—like fingerprint and facial recognition—lower the possibility of fraud and identity theft. Artificial intelligence (AI) algorithms and advanced data analytics aid in detecting and preventing suspicious transactions, guaranteeing adherence to legal requirements and protecting against illegal activity. Streamlined KYC procedures make faster account opening and verification possible, enhancing user satisfaction and lowering friction in remittance transactions.

Furthermore, new cross-border transfers and remittances developments are fueled by alliances and cooperation among financial institutions, tech firms, and regulatory agencies. The Financial Action Task Force (FATF) and the Global Remittance Alliance (GRA) are two initiatives supporting standardization and collaboration in the remittance sector, promoting interoperability and confidence among stakeholders. Fintech startups can test novel solutions in a controlled environment thanks to regulatory sandboxes and pilot programs, encouraging experimentation and advancing industry-wide innovation.

Despite the significant progress, it's important to acknowledge the challenges that persist in the remittance and cross-border transfer markets. Regulatory compliance, particularly with regard to anti-money laundering (AML) and counter-terrorism financing (CTF) regulations, remains a major concern. Another challenge is ensuring compatibility and interoperability across various platforms and payment systems, especially in areas with dispersed financial infrastructures. Maximizing the advantages of innovative remittance solutions for all stakeholders also requires addressing issues of financial literacy, accessibility, and trust.

In summary, advancements in remittances and cross-border transfers have revolutionized sending and receiving money across borders, providing migrants and their families with more convenient, affordable, and practical options. The remittance industry has undergone a revolution, becoming more efficient, secure, and inclusive thanks to digital remittance platforms, blockchain technology, mobile money services, and sophisticated identity verification procedures. To overcome the remaining obstacles and realize the full potential of digital remittances for worldwide financial inclusion and economic development, stakeholders must continue to collaborate and innovate.

CHAPTER III

Blockchain and Cryptocurrencies

Basics of blockchain technology

Blockchain technology has become a ground-breaking invention with significant ramifications for many industries, especially the financial sector. Fundamentally, blockchain is a distributed, decentralized ledger system that facilitates safe, open transactions without intermediaries. The notion of blockchain was initially presented in 2008 as the underlying technology of the cryptocurrency Bitcoin by an unidentified individual or group going by the name Satoshi Nakamoto. Since then, supply chain management, voting systems, and medical records are just a few of the many uses for blockchain technology beyond virtual currencies.

The core idea behind blockchain is that a network of connected nodes maintains a shared ledger of transactions. The blockchain comprises a series of blocks connected chronologically by the cryptographic hash of each previous block. Because any change to a single block would require the agreement of most network users, this cryptographic linking ensures the integrity and immutability of the data stored on the blockchain, making it highly resistant to fraud and tampering.

In the case of cryptocurrencies like Bitcoin, the backbone of the blockchain is the network users known as miners. These miners are responsible for recording and verifying transactions on the blockchain. Their role is crucial, as a new block can only be added to the blockchain by the first miner to solve a challenging mathematical puzzle. This competitive process, known as the proof-of-work consensus mechanism, ensures the safe and transparent validation and addition of transactions to the blockchain. It's important to note that other consensus techniques exist, such as proof-of-stake and delegated proof-of-stake, each with advantages and disadvantages.

Decentralization is one of the main characteristics of blockchain technology. Blockchain works on a peer-to-peer network where each node maintains a copy of the ledger, unlike traditional centralized systems where data is stored and managed by a single authority. Because blockchain technology is distributed, it does not require intermediaries or centralized authorities, which lowers the possibility of censorship and single points of failure. Because all transactions are recorded on a public ledger accessible to anybody with an internet connection, decentralization also improves accountability and transparency.

Transparency is a key feature of blockchain technology. Every transaction on the blockchain is instantly visible to every member of the network, as it is entered into a public ledger. This transparency is not just a feature, but a powerful tool that promotes user trust. Users can independently confirm the accuracy and integrity of the data without relying on third parties, which enhances accountability. Another significant feature of blockchain is the tamper-proof audit trail of transactions, which is invaluable for compliance, auditing, and dispute resolution.

One of the main concerns with blockchain technology is security. Blockchain's use of cryptographic algorithms and consensus procedures guarantees that transactions are safe and impervious to fraud or tampering. By distributing data among several nodes, the decentralized structure of blockchain further improves security by increasing the difficulty of network compromise by malevolent actors. Additionally, secure authentication and transaction encryption are made possible by using public and private key cryptography, guaranteeing that only individuals with the proper authorization can view and alter the data stored on the blockchain.

Blockchain technology has many benefits, but it also has drawbacks and restrictions. Scalability is a big concern because most blockchain networks' current architecture restricts the number of transactions that can be processed simultaneously. Congestion and delays have resulted from this, especially when there is a high transaction volume. Furthermore, calls for more energy-efficient alternatives have been sparked by the energy consumption of proof-of-work consensus mechanisms, like those used in Bitcoin mining, which has raised environmental concerns.

Standardization and interoperability present severe obstacles in the blockchain space as well. With thousands of blockchain initiatives and protocols in use, interoperability and communication across various networks remain challenging. The decentralized nature of the blockchain ecosystem has slowed progress in efforts to create interoperability standards and protocols. Moreover, regulatory ambiguity and noncompliance concerns impede the extensive integration of blockchain technology, especially in highly regulated sectors like banking and healthcare.

In summary, blockchain technology is a revolutionary paradigm shift in data transmission, verification, and storage. Because of its decentralized, transparent, and secure features, it has the potential to upend established markets and give people more control over their digital assets and transactions. However, to fully realize the transformative potential of blockchain technology across various sectors, issues like scalability, interoperability, and regulatory compliance need to be resolved. As technology develops and matures further, a new era of innovation and digital empowerment will begin.

Bitcoin and major cryptocurrencies

Unveiled in 2008 by an enigmatic figure or group known as Satoshi Nakamoto, Bitcoin stands as the pioneering decentralized digital currency in human history. This revolutionary concept allows users to conduct direct transactions, bypassing the need for traditional financial institutions. Operating on a peer-to-peer network, Bitcoin eliminates the middlemen, such as banks or governments, that typically oversee financial transactions. The underlying technology, blockchain, records these transactions on an open, transparent, and irreversible public ledger, ensuring their security and integrity.

Since its launch, Bitcoin's value and popularity have increased dramatically, making it one of the most well-known and frequently traded cryptocurrencies worldwide. Its decentralized structure, supply cap of 21 million coins, and pseudonymous transactions have drawn interest from investors looking for a different store of value to offset their holdings of conventional fiat currencies. However, there has been discussion about Bitcoin's price volatility, with large swings resulting in both large profits and losses for investors.

Many alternative cryptocurrencies, or altcoins, have surfaced in addition to Bitcoin, each with unique characteristics and applications. One of the most well-known cryptocurrencies is Ethereum, which was introduced by Vitalik Buterin in 2015. It is famous for its innovative contract feature, which lets programmers create autonomous organizations (DAOs) and decentralized applications (DApps) on its blockchain. Ether (ETH), the native cryptocurrency of Ethereum, powers network transactions and brilliant contract execution.

Other well-known cryptocurrencies are Cardano (ADA), a blockchain platform that emphasizes scalability, interoperability, and sustainability; Litecoin (LTC), sometimes referred to as the silver to Bitcoin's gold, which offers faster transaction times and lower fees; and Ripple (XRP), which seeks to enable quick and inexpensive cross-border payments for banks and financial institutions. These and other cryptocurrencies have become popular due to their unique characteristics and potential to upend several sectors outside of finance.

The emergence of cryptocurrencies has been full of difficulties and disputes. Governments and traditional financial institutions have expressed skepticism and caution towards the industry due to its problems with illicit activities, security breaches, and uncertain regulations. Global regulatory bodies have struggled to categorize and control cryptocurrencies; while some nations have accepted them as tangible financial assets, others have placed tight restrictions or outright bans on them.

Despite these obstacles, institutional investors' growing interest in cryptocurrencies, technological advancements, and changing consumer preferences drive their continued adoption. For supply chain management, asset tokenization, and payment processing, big financial institutions and businesses are starting to investigate blockchain and cryptocurrency-based solutions. Incorporating cryptocurrencies into traditional finance is considered a significant turning point in the continuous development of the digital economy.

Furthermore, the decentralized finance (DeFi) movement is gaining traction by utilizing blockchain technology to develop cutting-edge financial services and products that operate independently of conventional banking institutions. DeFi platforms provide more financial autonomy and inclusivity by allowing users to borrow, trade, and earn cryptocurrency interest without intermediaries. DeFi is not risk-free, though, as flaws in liquidity pools and intelligent contracts can result in security lapses and monetary losses.

Prospects for Bitcoin and other prominent cryptocurrencies are bright but uncertain. Continued innovation and growth in cryptocurrency will likely be fueled by regulatory clarity, widespread adoption, and technological advancements. The full potential of blockchain technology and cryptocurrencies will require addressing issues like scalability, privacy, and sustainability. Bitcoin and other major cryptocurrencies have the potential to significantly alter the financial landscape and empower people all over the world as the digital economy develops.

Applications of blockchain in financial services

Created as the foundation for Bitcoin, blockchain technology has matured into a flexible instrument with various uses in various sectors, most notably finance. Blockchain is a decentralized, unchangeable technology that can improve financial processes and transactions' efficiency, security, and transparency. Financial institutions and fintech firms are investigating and deploying blockchain-based solutions more frequently to improve operations, cut expenses, and lower risks.

Payment and remittance systems are among the most notable uses of blockchain technology in the financial services industry. With blockchain, cross-border payments may be made almost instantly without middlemen like banks or money transfer services. The blockchain-based payment technology known as Ripple has gained popularity because it makes cross-border transactions for banks and other financial institutions quick and affordable. By utilizing blockchain technology, payment networks can decrease transaction costs, shorten settlement times, and improve transparency in cross-border money transfers.

Blockchain in supply chain management and trade finance is another critical application. The decentralized ledger of blockchain technology offers a safe and impenetrable transaction record, facilitating increased supply chain transparency and traceability. Trade finance participants can access real-time information and trace the flow of commodities along the supply chain by digitizing trade papers, such as bills of lading, invoices, and purchase orders, and storing them on a blockchain. This increases efficiency and mutual trust among trading partners while lowering the danger of fraud, mistakes, and delays.

Blockchain has the potential to completely transform the settlement and trading of securities. Because several intermediaries and manual procedures are involved, traditional securities markets are sometimes beset by inefficiencies, excessive costs, and protracted settlement delays. Thanks to blockchain-based securities platforms like security token exchanges, digital securities can be issued, traded, and settled more quickly and transparently. Blockchain improves liquidity and accessibility in capital markets by enabling 24/7 trading, automating compliance checks, and lowering counterparty risk.

Furthermore, blockchain technology can democratize access to financial services. DeF through decentralized finance (DeFi) systems platforms are decentralized versions of standard financial services using blockchain and innovative contract technology, including lending, borrowing, trading, and asset management. Because no middlemen are involved, users can use these services straight from their digital wallets, increasing their financial inclusion and autonomy. Additionally, DeFi platforms facilitate financial solutions that are programmable and composable, giving customers the ability to tailor and optimize their economic plans.

Identity management solutions built on blockchain technology represent yet another financial services breakthrough. Conventional identification verification procedures are frequently unreliable, laborious, and fraud-prone. With blockchain-based identification systems, users may securely control and manage their digital identities on a decentralized network. By storing encrypted identification data on a blockchain, users can selectively release information to third parties while protecting their privacy and security. This lowers the possibility of identity theft, expedites the onboarding procedure, and improves regulatory compliance.

While blockchain offers numerous benefits for the financial services industry, it's not without its challenges. Issues with scalability, interoperability, and regulatory compliance persist. Blockchain networks require continuous research and development to handle large transaction volumes without compromising speed or security. Interoperability across various blockchain platforms and legacy systems is also a crucial factor for smooth adoption and integration. However, the broad implementation of blockchain-based solutions is hampered by regulatory ambiguity and compliance concerns, as financial institutions grapple with complex regulatory structures and compliance obligations.

Blockchain technology presents a wealth of opportunities for financial services to innovate and transform. Its potential to revolutionize various financial processes and operations, from identity management to trade finance, securities trading, payment and remittance systems, and decentralized finance, is immense. To fully harness this potential, financial institutions, regulators, and stakeholders must collaborate to overcome challenges and pave the way for blockchain's transformative journey in reshaping the financial industry as the technology evolves and matures.

CHAPTER IV

Robo-Advisors and Wealth Management

Definition and function of robo-advisors

Robo-advisors, unlike traditional financial advisors, are automated investing systems. They manage client accounts and offer individualized financial advice using computer and algorithmic algorithms. These digital platforms, which use technology to evaluate financial data, determine risk tolerance, and suggest diverse investment plans, provide a unique and cost-effective alternative to conventional human financial advisors. To provide investment recommendations that are specific to each client's objectives, time horizon, and risk tolerance, robo-advisors often combine contemporary portfolio theory, machine learning algorithms, and human input.

Robo-advisors are designed to simplify the investing process and give customers easy access to professionally managed portfolios without requiring human involvement. After a straightforward online risk assessment and registration process, clients can receive individualized investment recommendations that are tailored to their risk tolerance and financial objectives. Next, using algorithms, robo-advisors distribute their clients' money among a variety of assets, including bonds, equities, exchange-traded funds (ETFs), and other financial goods.

Compared to traditional wealth management services, robo-advisors offer many benefits, such as lower fees, enhanced accessibility, and increased transparency. Robo-advisors automate the investment process, enabling them to provide wealth management services at a significantly lower cost than traditional financial advisors. This accessibility to wealth management benefits a broader spectrum of clients, including millennials and those with smaller investment portfolios. Furthermore, robo-advisors give customers round-the-clock access to their performance information and investment accounts, increasing transparency and enabling them to make wise financial decisions.

Offering services for tax-loss harvesting and portfolio rebalancing is another vital role of robo-advisors. Rebalancing a portfolio entails modifying its asset allocation regularly to preserve the intended risk-return profile. Robo-advisors use algorithms to monitor market circumstances and automatically adjust customers' portfolios when needed to keep them in line with their investing goals. Tax-loss harvesting is a tactic where underperforming investments are sold, and profits are offset with losses to reduce taxes on investment gains. Robo-advisors can use tax-loss harvesting algorithms to minimize their clients' tax obligations and enhance their post-tax profits.

To assist clients in reaching their long-term financial objectives, robo-advisors also provide goal-based investment services and individualized financial planning.

Robo-advisors allow clients to define specific financial goals, such as wealth accumulation, retirement savings, or funding for school, and they suggest investment strategies based on those goals. Clients can monitor their progress toward their financial goals through goal-based investing and modify them to stay on course.

To help clients minimize investment risk and optimize returns, robo-advisors also offer risk management and portfolio optimization tools. Robo-advisors can use sophisticated algorithms and historical data analysis to determine their client's risk tolerance and suggest the proper asset allocations to attain the best risk-adjusted returns. To improve portfolio performance and reduce downside risk, robo-advisors can also employ machine learning algorithms to assess market movements and modify investing methods continuously.

While robo-advisors offer many advantages, it's important to consider their limitations. While they are easily accessible and convenient, they might not provide the same level of individualized care and human interaction as traditional financial advisors. Confident investors might prefer the counsel and experience of a human advisor, particularly in times of market turbulence or noteworthy life events. Furthermore, high-net-worth individuals with sophisticated investment strategies or extensive financial planning needs might not find robo-advisors to be the best fit.

In summary, robo-advisors are automated investing systems that manage client portfolios and offer individualized financial advice using computer and algorithmic algorithms. By utilizing technology to streamline the investment process and give clients access to professionally managed portfolios, these digital platforms present a practical and affordable substitute for traditional wealth management services. Personalized financial planning services, accessibility, transparency, and reduced fees are benefits of using robo-advisors. They may only be appropriate for some investors, though, and some prefer the advice and experience of a human financial advisor. Robo-advisors are critical to democratizing wealth management and enabling investors to reach their financial objectives more effectively and efficiently.

How AI is transforming wealth management

By utilizing sophisticated algorithms and data analytics to improve decision-making, automate procedures, and customize financial advice for customers, artificial intelligence (AI) is completely changing the wealth management industry. Wealth managers can now examine massive volumes of economic data, spot patterns, and trends, and quickly produce actionable insights thanks to artificial intelligence (AI) technologies like machine learning, natural language processing, and predictive analytics. Wealth management companies are changing due to this shift, which allows them to provide clients with more individualized, effective, and efficient services.

Data-driven investing strategies are one of the main ways AI revolutionizes wealth management. AI-powered algorithms can examine past market data, economic indicators, and investor sentiment to find possible investments and forecast market trends. By utilizing machine learning techniques, wealth managers can create complex investment models that adjust and change over time in response to shifting market conditions. As a result, they may maximize portfolio performance for customers and make better-informed investment decisions.

Furthermore, thanks to AI, wealth managers can now provide individualized financial suggestions and guidance based on each client's particular needs and objectives. AI algorithms can produce personalized investment strategies and asset allocations that correspond with clients' preferences by evaluating their financial profiles, risk tolerance, and investment objectives. By enabling wealth managers to communicate with customers in real-time via chatbots and virtual assistants, responding to queries instantly, and offering tailored financial advice, natural language processing technologies further improve the client experience.

AI is also revolutionizing risk management in wealth management companies. Wealth managers can proactively detect and manage potential risks in their customers' investment portfolios by utilizing machine learning algorithms and predictive analytics. Risk management systems driven by AI can track changes in the market, identify irregularities, and notify wealth managers of possible risks to their customers' investments. This makes it possible for wealth managers to minimize downside risk and safeguard clients' assets proactively.

AI is also revolutionizing the wealth management industry's customer onboarding and account management procedures. Wealth managers may expedite the onboarding process for new customers, minimize paperwork, and streamline account opening procedures by utilizing automation solutions driven by artificial intelligence. Wealth managers may onboard customers more quickly and ensure regulatory compliance by using natural language processing algorithms to automate the evaluation and analysis of client documents, including financial statements and risk assessment questionnaires.

AI is also helping wealth managers improve client happiness and engagement by facilitating individualized communications and financial literacy programs. By examining clients' financial habits and preferences, artificial intelligence algorithms can collect recommendations and material specific to the morals and interests of health managers, may improve the client experience, and build lasting relationships by using AI-powered chatbots and virtual assistants to give clients individualized financial advice, real-time question answers, and educational materials.

Even with AI's advantages for wealth management, there are still issues, especially with data security, privacy, and regulatory compliance. Strict regulations, including the GDPR and CCPA, require wealth management companies to maintain robust data protection protocols to protect their clients' sensitive financial information. The ethical ramifications of AI-powered decision-making in wealth management, such as algorithmic bias and transparency, must be adequately studied and handled to preserve integrity and confidence in the sector.

In conclusion, AI is revolutionizing the wealth management industry by allowing managers to use sophisticated algorithms and data analytics to improve decision-making, streamline workflows, and provide clients with individualized financial advice. AI is changing how wealth management companies run and provide services to their clients in several ways, including risk management, individualized financial advising, data-driven investment strategies, and client interaction. Even though there are still obstacles to overcome, AI has enormous potential to improve wealth management in the digital age by increasing productivity, efficacy, and client satisfaction.

Case studies of leading robo-advisors

Robo-advisors, which provide automated, algorithm-driven financial planning services with little human participation, have entirely transformed the wealth management sector. The need for affordable, easily accessible investment advice and management has propelled their growth. This essay examines the characteristics, business strategies, and effects of some popular robo-advisors, such as Betterment, Wealthfront, and Vanguard Personal Advisor Services, on the financial services industry.

Founded in 2008, Betterment is frequently recognized as a trailblazer in the robo-advisory field. The platform's user-friendly interface is intended to deliver personalized investment management and guidance. Betterment's primary product is its goal-based investing framework, which assists users in establishing and accomplishing monetary objectives like saving for retirement or purchasing a property. The platform creates diversified portfolios that align with the client's risk tolerance and time horizon by combining inexpensive exchange-traded funds (ETFs). Betterment's tax-loss harvesting service automatically sells lost investments to offset profits and reduce tax burden is one of its standout features. Those who own taxable accounts and want to improve their after-tax returns have found this service especially intriguing. Additionally, Betterment provides a premium plan with access to qualified financial advisors for more individualized guidance. Betterment's success has cleared the Path for more industry advances while proving that fully automated financial advising services are feasible.

Another significant participant in the robo-advisory space, Wealthfront, was established in 2011 and immediately became well-known for its technologically advanced approach to investment management. The platform offered by Wealthfront uses cutting-edge algorithms to generate customized investment plans according to its clients' risk tolerance and financial objectives. Wealthfront builds client portfolios using a diverse mix of exchange-traded funds (ETFs), much like Betterment. However, Wealthfront sets itself apart with several extra tools to provide users with a whole financial planning experience. One noteworthy element is Wealthfront's financial planning tool, Path, which tracks clients' progress toward objectives like homeownership or retirement using real-time data.

Additionally, Wealthfront provides a sophisticated tax optimization method that enables clients to own individual stocks and optimize at a granular level for tax efficiency. This strategy includes tax-loss harvesting and direct indexing. In addition, Wealthfront offers a cash management account with the option to automate saves and receive a high-interest return on cash deposits. Wealthfront has established itself as a comprehensive financial platform by offering a wide range of services that address more than simply investment management.

The Vanguard Personal Advisor Services (VPAS) concept is a hybrid that blends the advantages of robo-advisors with the knowledge and experience of human financial advisors. VPAS, a personalized financial plan established by human advisors and managed by automated technology, was introduced by Vanguard, one of the world's biggest and most reputable investment management organizations. By combining the scalability and cost-effectiveness of robo-advisors with the individualized, nuanced guidance that human advisors can provide. Clients fill out an online form to determine their financial objectives, risk tolerance, and time horizon. Vanguard advisors create a personalized financial strategy based on this data, which is then implemented with inexpensive Vanguard funds. Automation handles the continuing portfolio management, including tax efficiency plans and rebalancing, ensuring that customers' assets stay in line with their financial objectives over time. Additionally, VPAS gives customers ongoing access to human advisors for more complicated financial inquiries or life events that can impact their investment plan.

The financial services sector is shifting towards technology-driven solutions that promote accessibility, cost efficiency, and personalization. This is exemplified by the success of these prominent robo-advisors. Wealthfront and Betterment's fully automated models have shown that high-end investment management may be provided for a small portion of the price of conventional financial advice services. Vanguard Personal Advisor Services' hybrid model demonstrates how fusing automated technology with human knowledge may provide a compelling value proposition for clients looking for a more individualized touch.

These case studies demonstrate the variety of strategies used in the robo-advisory market and emphasize how the sector is still developing. Robo-advisors are expected to become more important in wealth management as technology evolves and investor tastes move toward digital solutions. Their capacity to democratize access to expert investment management and advice has the potential to completely change the financial services industry by opening up high-quality financial planning to a hitherto untapped market.

CHAPTER V

Regulatory and Compliance Issues

Overview of financial regulations

Financial laws depend heavily on the integrity, stability, and reliability of the world's financial systems. These laws cover various guidelines and norms intended to control markets, financial institutions, and transactions to safeguard consumers, maintain honest competition, and reduce systemic risks. Financial rules have changed due to technological breakthroughs, economic growth, and financial crises. As a result, financial institutions now have to negotiate a complicated regulatory environment.

The Basel Accords, created by the Basel Committee on Banking Supervision (BCBS), are one of the main regulatory frameworks. Basel I, Basel II, and Basel III are international rules for banking regulation that address market liquidity risk, stress testing, and capital adequacy. Basel III was enacted after the 2008 financial crisis to strengthen bank resilience and lower the probability of future economic crises. It introduced stricter capital requirements, leverage ratios, and liquidity restrictions. These rules guarantee that banks have enough capital reserves to cover losses and carry on business during hard times.

One of the most extensive financial regulation reforms in recent memory was implemented in the United States in 2010 with the passage of the Dodd-Frank Wall Street Reform and Consumer Protection Act. Through strengthening regulatory control of financial institutions, expanding consumer rights, and lowering systemic risk, the Dodd-Frank Act sought to address the root causes of the 2008 financial crisis. The Financial Stability Oversight

Council (FSOC) was established to keep an eye on systemic risks; the Consumer Financial Protection Bureau (CFPB) was established to shield consumers from deceptive financial practices; and the Volcker Rule, which limits bank investments and proprietary trading, are some of the main features of the Dodd-Frank Act.

Both national laws and EU-wide directives and regulations influence the financial regulatory environment in Europe. The European Union's financial markets and investment services are primarily governed by the Markets in Financial Instruments Directive (MiFID) and MiFID II. When MiFID II was implemented in 2018, it brought stringent rules for transparency, investor safeguards, and increased reporting duties for financial institutions. By guaranteeing a high degree of investor protection and upholding market integrity, the directive seeks to establish a more cohesive and effective financial market throughout the EU.

The General Data Protection Regulation (GDPR) is another critical legal framework in Europe that went into effect in 2018. GDPR's strict data protection and privacy standards, even if not just financial legislation, have significant consequences for financial organizations. GDPR requires businesses to have strong data protection measures, get express consent before processing personal data, and give people more control over their personal information. Data protection is a crucial compliance concern for financial institutions operating in the EU, as non-compliance with GDPR can result in significant fines.

Regulations about counter-terrorist financing (CTF) and anti-money laundering (AML) are essential worldwide for averting financial crimes and preserving the economic system's stability. Member nations of the Financial Action Task Force (FATF), an intergovernmental organization, must enact national laws to carry out the international standards for AML and CTF measures. Financial institutions must conduct due diligence on their customers, monitor transactions for unusual activity, and notify the appropriate authorities of suspicious activities. Maintaining confidence in the economic system and stopping illegal actions like money laundering and financing terrorism depend on compliance with AML and CTF legislation.

Financial institutions are subject to several additional regulations unique to their operations and countries in addition to these frameworks. Among them are laws governing exchanges and securities, such as the Securities Act of 1933 and the Securities Exchange Act of 1934 in the US, which control the issue and trading of securities and mandate that investors be informed of relevant information. Through capital requirements, lending rules, and supervisory reviews, prudential regulations—such as those upheld by the Federal Reserve and the Office of the Comptroller of the Currency (OCC) in the United States—ensure the safety and soundness of banks.

The swift progression of technology in fintech and digital assets brings forth novel regulatory prospects and obstacles. Regulators are paying increasing attention to mitigating the dangers posed by cutting-edge technology like blockchain, cryptocurrency, and artificial intelligence. As a result, frameworks for rules about digital assets, cybersecurity, and data governance are changing. To safeguard investors and maintain market integrity, the European Union proposes the Markets in Crypto-Assets Regulation (MiCA), establishing a uniform regulatory framework for cryptocurrencies and digital assets.

Financial regulations are critical to preserving the integrity, stability, and reliability of the world financial system. These laws cover various guidelines and requirements, including capital adequacy, consumer protection, openness, and anti-money laundering protocols. Regulations must change to meet new risks and possibilities as the financial sector develops. This keeps financial institutions operating safely and effectively, safeguarding customers and upholding market integrity. For financial institutions to reduce risks, stay out of trouble, and maintain the confidence of both their customers and the more extensive financial system, they must adhere to financial rules.

Regulatory challenges for Fintech companies

The financial services industry has seen a significant transformation due to the swift development of fintech, or financial technology, which has brought about novel approaches that improve user experience, efficiency, and accessibility. Fintech businesses must carefully navigate many regulatory obstacles as they push the limits of traditional finance. These issues include consumer protection, cybersecurity, data privacy, anti-money laundering (AML), and the difficulties of conducting business in several jurisdictions with various regulatory frameworks.

A primary regulatory obstacle for fintech enterprises is guaranteeing adherence to data protection regulations. Strict data protection regulations must be followed since fintech solutions rely significantly on gathering and analyzing user data. The collection, processing, and storage of personal data are subject to strict regulations, such as the General Data Protection Regulation (GDPR) of the European Union. These rules give people much control over their personal information and require express agreement from users. Complying with these standards requires fintech organizations to invest heavily in safe data storage solutions and create procedures to deal with data breaches as soon as they occur. Data privacy is essential because noncompliance can result in hefty fines and harm the company's reputation.

Another significant regulatory difficulty for financial companies is cybersecurity. Fintech services are digital; thus, they are vulnerable to cyberattacks that could compromise private financial information and cause service disruptions. Global regulatory agencies progressively require robust cybersecurity frameworks to fend off these attacks. For instance, extensive cybersecurity standards have been set by the New York State Department of Financial Services (NYDFS) for financial institutions, including fintech businesses. Implementing thorough cybersecurity programs, conducting frequent risk assessments, and reporting incidents are mandated by these requirements. Fintech companies must continually invest in technology and qualified staff to maintain compliance. They must also upgrade their security protocols and remain alert to changing cyber threats.

Another major compliance issue facing fintech companies, particularly those engaged in payments, money transfers, and digital currencies, is the enforcement of anti-money laundering (AML) legislation. By mandating institutions to monitor transactions and report unusual activity, anti-money laundering (AML) regulations aim to prevent financial crimes. The Financial Action Task Force (FATF) establishes global anti-money laundering (AML) guidelines, which its member nations enact into national laws. Fintech businesses need to create complex AML processes that include transaction monitoring, customer due diligence (CDD), and reporting of suspicious conduct. Identifying odd patterns suggestive of money laundering frequently entails integrating cutting-edge technologies like artificial intelligence and machine learning. Maintaining regulatory approval and preventing illicit operations require efficient AML compliance.

Another issue is the occurrence of regulatory arbitrage, in which businesses take advantage of variations in laws between different countries. Fintech companies frequently have a global presence, and navigating the many regulatory frameworks can be challenging. The legal systems of several nations can occasionally contradict one another. For example, a fintech business that operates in the EU and the US has to abide by GDPR in the EU and the less strict data privacy rules in the US. Due to this discrepancy, fintech companies must adapt their operations to satisfy the most stringent regulatory requirements in every country they service, which raises the bar for compliance and increases costs.

Regulations about consumer protection are crucial for fintech businesses. These rules guarantee that financial services and products are equitable and transparent and do not exploit customers. Financial services are regulated by organizations such as the Consumer Financial Protection Bureau (CFPB) in the US to shield customers against deceptive business practices. Fintech businesses must ensure conditions are communicated, prices are transparent, and customer funds are protected. It can be challenging to balance innovation and consumer safety when fintech companies try to provide innovative solutions while abiding by laws meant to safeguard customers.

The rapid advancement of fintech has resulted in regulatory unpredictability. Regulators typically face challenges in keeping up with the emergence of new technologies such as blockchain, cryptocurrencies, and artificial intelligence. Due to this delay, fintech businesses operate in an uncertain environment since they can encounter sudden changes in regulations or heightened scrutiny. This problem is best illustrated by how cryptocurrencies are regulated; while some nations embrace digital assets, others have tight laws or outright prohibitions. Fintech businesses that deal with cryptocurrencies must remain flexible and adaptive to survive in this unstable regulatory environment.

In summary, as fintech businesses develop and grow, they must navigate complex regulatory issues. It takes significant resources and careful preparation to ensure compliance with data privacy laws, cybersecurity standards, AML regulations, and consumer protection obligations. Additionally, fintech companies must be proactive and agile to manage regulatory arbitrage and navigate regulatory uncertainty. Fintech companies can overcome these difficulties and create a regulatory climate that promotes innovation while maintaining the stability and integrity of the financial system by investing in solid compliance processes and cooperating with regulators.

Global regulatory frameworks and their impact

International regulatory frameworks significantly impact how financial systems and economic stability are developed in various nations. These frameworks are intended to safeguard consumers, stop financial crimes, guarantee the stability and soundness of financial institutions, and advance equity and transparency in the financial markets. These regulatory frameworks significantly impact how financial institutions function, manage risks, and interact with customers and markets worldwide.

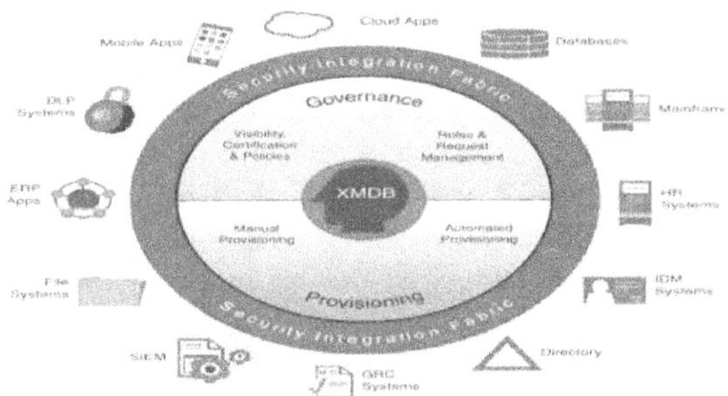

The Basel Committee on Banking Supervision (BCBS) created the Basel Accords, one of the most critical international regulatory frameworks. These agreements, which include Basel I, Basel II, and Basel III, establish global guidelines for regulating banks about market liquidity risk, stress testing, and capital adequacy. Basel III has significantly impacted the banking industry which was implemented in reaction to the 2008 financial crisis. With the introduction of stricter capital requirements, leverage ratios, and liquidity coverage ratios, banks worldwide are now required to keep larger capital buffers and more effective risk management procedures in place. By strengthening banks' resistance to economic shocks, these steps hope to lessen the chance of further financial crises. Nevertheless, banks now face more compliance costs due to the heavier regulatory load, which may impact their profitability and capacity to compete.

The European Union's financial markets have been significantly impacted by the securities regulations about securities, particularly by the Markets in Financial Instruments Directive (MiFID) and its successor, MiFID II. When MiFID II was implemented in 2018, it brought stringent rules for transparency, investor safeguards, and increased reporting duties for financial institutions. By guaranteeing a high degree of investor protection and upholding market integrity, these regulations seek to establish a more cohesive and effective financial market throughout the EU. Financial institutions had to redesign their trading and reporting systems to comply with MiFID II, which resulted in high compliance costs. But it has also enhanced the quality of financial goods and advice accessible to investors, decreased conflicts of interest, and boosted market transparency.

One of the most extensive financial regulation reforms in recent memory was accomplished in the United States in 2010 with the passage of the Dodd-Frank Wall Street Reform and Consumer Protection Act. In reaction to the

2008 financial crisis, this legislation was presented with the goals of strengthening financial institution regulatory monitoring, enhancing consumer rights, and lowering systemic risk. The Financial Stability Oversight Council (FSOC) was established to keep an eye on systemic risks; the Consumer Financial Protection Bureau (CFPB) was established to shield consumers from deceptive financial practices; and the Volcker Rule, which limits bank investments and proprietary trading, are some of the main features of the Dodd-Frank Act. The Dodd-Frank Act has dramatically altered the regulatory environment in the United States. This has resulted in heightened oversight and inspection of financial institutions, influencing their operating strategies and risk management procedures.

The General Data Protection Regulation (GDPR), enacted by the European Union in 2018, is another critical legal framework with worldwide consequences. GDPR imposes strict guidelines for data security and privacy that apply to EU-based and non-EU businesses that handle the personal data of EU citizens. For financial firms that manage enormous volumes of sensitive personal data, GDPR has significant ramifications. GDPR compliance necessitates a substantial investment in data protection measures, such as safe data storage, procedures for notifying individuals of data breaches, and methods for getting individuals' express consent to process their data. Data privacy is a crucial compliance concern for financial organizations worldwide since non-compliance can lead to hefty fines.

The global regulatory system also includes anti-money laundering (AML) and counter-terrorist financing (CTF) legislation, which are essential. Member nations enact national laws to implement the worldwide standards for AML and CTF procedures established by the Financial Action Task Force (FATF). Global financial institutions must follow these guidelines by putting vital AML programs in place, checking customers thoroughly, and checking for unusual activity in transactions. Maintaining the economic system's integrity and preventing financial crimes require strict adherence to AML and CTF requirements. Financial institutions must invest in cutting-edge technologies and qualified staff to successfully detect and prevent unlawful activity, which puts enormous operating and compliance costs on them.

Global regulatory frameworks impact more than operational adjustments and compliance costs. They also influence the financial sector's competitive dynamics. Stricter laws might result in more entrance barriers, particularly for smaller businesses that need more resources to comply with the standards. On the other hand, they can also level the playing field by ensuring that everyone in the market follows the same rules, encouraging fair competition and lowering the likelihood of financial misbehavior.

Global regulatory frameworks also support investor confidence and financial stability. Thanks to these frameworks' strict rules for capital adequacy, risk management, and transparency, systemic risks are reduced, and economic crises are avoided. Additionally, they strengthen investor protection by guaranteeing customers can obtain honest and open financial services and products. Consequently, this promotes confidence in the economic system, which is necessary for its seamless operation and expansion.

In summary, international regulatory frameworks significantly influence the financial industry, influencing how businesses function, handle risks, and interact with customers and markets. These rules encourage economic stability, openness, and justice even if they present substantial operational and compliance expenses. To safeguard consumers and preserve the financial system's integrity, regulatory frameworks must change to meet

new risks and opportunities as the economic landscape
develops.

57

CHAPTER VI

Cybersecurity and Data Privacy

Importance of cybersecurity in Fintech

Cybersecurity has become essential to upholding confidence and guaranteeing the integrity of digital financial services in the quickly developing fintech industry. The smooth and secure transmission of economic data is critical to the fintech industry, which includes technologies like peer-to-peer lending, digital payments, blockchain, and robo-advisors. Strong cybersecurity measures are therefore necessary to safeguard confidential information, stop financial fraud, and maintain customer trust.

Given the significant risks involved, the significance of cybersecurity in the financial industry cannot be emphasized. Because financial transactions and services involve large sums of money and sensitive data, cybercriminals often target them. Data breaches in the fintech industry can seriously harm firms' and consumers' reputations and result in significant financial losses. Robust cybersecurity procedures are essential for reducing these risks and protecting users' financial and personal data, which is essential for preserving the economic system's integrity.

Safeguarding sensitive financial data is one of the most critical components of cybersecurity in the fintech industry. Fintech businesses manage vast personal data, such as credit card numbers, bank account information, and transaction history. Cybercriminals frequently use this data as a target for fraud, identity theft, and other nefarious acts. Fintech organizations may lower the risk of data breaches by putting multi-factor authentication, advanced encryption techniques, and secure data storage systems into place. These safeguards protect consumers from financial risk by ensuring that, even if data is intercepted, it remains unreadable and unusable to unauthorized parties.

Furthermore, combating financial fraud in the fintech industry depends on cybersecurity. Fintech services are digital, making them handy, but they also allow hackers to exploit weaknesses. Cybercriminals frequently use tactics like phishing, which involves tricking people into disclosing personal information. Fintech organizations must implement robust fraud detection and prevention systems using artificial intelligence and machine learning to detect and stop suspicious activity in real-time. By doing this, businesses can safeguard their clients from fraud and uphold the confidence necessary for the general acceptance of fintech solutions.

The regulatory landscape is another factor that makes cybersecurity essential to fintech. Globally, governments and regulatory agencies have instituted strict cybersecurity and data protection policies to protect customers and preserve financial stability. For example, the General Data Protection Regulation (GDPR) of the European Union places stringent limitations on how businesses gather, handle, and retain personal data. Similarly, the New York Department of Financial Services (NYDFS) has implemented strict cybersecurity rules, especially for financial institutions. These regulations must be followed; not doing so may result in fines, legal ramifications, and reputational harm to the business. Fintech businesses must thus prioritize cybersecurity to comply with regulations and avoid the dire repercussions of non-compliance.

Another critical factor is how cybersecurity events may affect FinTech's brand. The base upon which financial services are constructed is trust. Customers need to feel confident knowing that fintech services are reliable for their banking, investing, and payment needs and the security of their financial information. A cybersecurity breach can damage this trust, resulting in a decline in market share, a loss of clients, and long-term harm to the company's reputation. Fintech organizations may cultivate trust and loyalty among their user base by demonstrating their commitment to safeguarding consumer data and upholding the highest security standards through proactive investment in robust cybersecurity solutions.

Cybersecurity is essential for managing internal risks and defending against external attacks. Insider threats represent a severe risk to fintech companies, regardless of their motive. Workers or contractors who have access to private information may misuse it for their benefit or may carelessly expose it without meaning to. Insider threat risk can be reduced by putting strong access controls in place, conducting frequent security training, and keeping a close eye on user activity. Fintech organizations can protect themselves from internal vulnerabilities by ensuring that only authorized workers have access to sensitive information and are aware of security best practices.

Furthermore, the whole financial ecosystem benefits from cybersecurity in the fintech sector. Fintech businesses frequently collaborate with other third-party service providers, payment processors, and conventional financial institutions. A single cybersecurity incident may have a domino effect that compromises the network as a whole. Fintech businesses must thus take a comprehensive approach to cybersecurity and ensure that their suppliers and partners follow strict security guidelines as well. Maintaining the general security and stability of the financial system depends on this cooperative effort.

Conclusively, the fintech business places great emphasis on cybersecurity because of the delicate nature of financial data, the elevated likelihood of financial fraud, the strict adherence to regulatory standards, and the imperative to uphold consumer confidence. By putting strong cybersecurity measures in place, fintech businesses may ensure regulatory compliance, safeguard user data, stop financial fraud, and maintain their brand. Dedication to cybersecurity will be essential to promoting innovation and guaranteeing the safe and secure provision of digital financial services as the fintech scene develops.

Common cybersecurity threats and solutions

Cybersecurity threats are a significant concern for individuals, corporations, and governments in the increasingly digital world. The growth of technology has brought about enormous benefits, but it has also generated new vulnerabilities that hackers are ready to exploit. Protecting sensitive data and maintaining the integrity of digital operations need an understanding of typical cybersecurity threats and the implementation of practical solutions.

One of the most common dangers to cybersecurity is phishing. It entails hackers disguising themselves as trustworthy organizations to trick people into disclosing private information such as credit card numbers, usernames, and passwords. Phishing assaults can happen through text messaging and social media, but they mainly occur via email. Frequently, the emails include malicious attachments or links that, when clicked, expose the victim's data. To tackle phishing, firms must adopt robust email filtering systems that recognize and block questionable messages. The likelihood of becoming a victim of these attacks can also be significantly decreased by teaching staff members and users how to spot phishing efforts and urging them to confirm the legitimacy of any unexpected requests for sensitive information. Another proper precaution is multi-factor authentication (MFA), which adds protection by requiring many verification forms before allowing access to accounts.

Ransomware is another significant threat, typified by malicious software that encrypts a victim's data and demands payment for its release. Attacks using ransomware have the potential to be disastrous, resulting in significant financial losses and delays to operations. To counter this threat, enterprises should frequently back up their data and ensure that these backups are maintained offline or in a secure cloud environment, making restoring data without paying the ransom feasible. It's also crucial to keep systems and software updated with the newest security updates because doing so can stop hackers from taking advantage of already-known vulnerabilities. A thorough defensive strategy must include implementing robust endpoint protection solutions and frequent security training for staff members to identify and steer clear of ransomware attack channels, such as dubious emails and downloads.

The availability of internet services is significantly at risk from distributed denial of service (DDoS) assaults. To render a target server, service, or network inoperable, these attacks entail flooding it with excessive internet traffic. A successful DDoS assault has the potential to have catastrophic effects, impairing company operations and seriously harming finances and reputation. Deploying DDoS protection services, which may absorb and filter out malicious data and ensure that genuine traffic still reaches its intended destination, is one way to combat DDoS attacks. Content delivery networks (CDNs) are another tool that enterprises can use to spread traffic loads and improve defenses against these kinds of attacks. Regularly upgrading and patching systems to close security holes and deploying network traffic monitoring to detect and respond to unexpected patterns might further help fight against DDoS attacks.

Malware is a large group of harmful software, including viruses, worms, trojans, and spyware. Malware can do significant harm by stealing data, interfering with system operations, or gaining unauthorized access to systems. Malware protection calls for a multi-layered strategy. Cutting-edge antivirus and anti-malware programs can identify and eliminate unwanted software before it does any damage. Frequent software updates and patches are essential for addressing security flaws that malicious software could exploit. In the event of an attack, network segmentation—which entails splitting a network into smaller, isolated segments—can stop malware from spreading. Strict access controls and frequent security audits to find and fix vulnerabilities are critical components of malware defense strategies.

Insider threats pose a serious concern to cybersecurity because they involve the malevolent or careless acts of workers or other trusted individuals. These dangers may lead to sensitive information theft, data breaches, or other adverse actions. Organizations should put strict access controls in place to ensure that only authorized individuals have access to sensitive data to reduce insider threats. Employees can identify and avoid harmful actions by participating in security awareness training and routinely monitoring user activities. Practical strategies to mitigate insider threats include conducting background checks on potential hires and putting data loss prevention (DLP) systems in place to monitor and restrict the movement of sensitive information.

Advanced Persistent Threats (APTs) are complex, protracted cyberattacks that steal data or cause long-term harm. APTs are usually carried out by highly proficient attackers, who frequently have substantial resources, like nation-state actors. These sneaky attacks employ various methods, such as bespoke malware, zero-day vulnerabilities, and social engineering. A proactive and all-encompassing cybersecurity strategy comprising threat intelligence, ongoing network monitoring, and sophisticated intrusion detection systems is needed to counteract APTs. To eliminate security flaws, organizations should also use a zero-trust security model that authenticates all network activity and regularly updates and patches their systems.

The proliferation of linked devices, many of which have inadequate security safeguards, makes the Internet of Things (IoT) a unique cybersecurity risk. IoT devices can be used as weapons, gather information, or breach networks. Robust authentication protocols, frequent firmware upgrades, and network segmentation to separate IoT devices from critical systems are necessary to secure IoT environments. Regular vulnerability evaluations and implementing security standards for IoT devices can also assist in reducing hazards.

In conclusion, a diversified strategy for protection is required due to the always-changing and complex landscape of cybersecurity threats. By understanding typical threats such as phishing, ransomware, DDoS assaults, malware, insider threats, APTs, and IoT vulnerabilities, businesses may develop practical solutions to defend their digital assets. To reduce these risks and guarantee the resilience and integrity of digital operations, a proactive security posture, ongoing monitoring, personnel education, and cutting-edge technology tools must be used in concert. Maintaining strong cybersecurity defenses requires remaining aware and adjusting security measures as cyber threats change.

Data privacy concerns and regulatory requirements

Data privacy has become a top priority for people, businesses, and governments everywhere in the current digital era. The exponential increase in the gathering, storing, and processing of personal information has resulted in severe privacy problems. Strong data privacy policies and regulatory compliance are more important than ever as technology develops, and data becomes increasingly essential to business operations.

The quantity of personal information that organizations gather, and the possibility of its misuse are the leading causes of data privacy concerns. Any information that may be used to identify a specific person, such as names, addresses, social security numbers, and financial information, is considered personal data. Due to the widespread use of social media and digital services, an unprecedented amount of data is being collected—often without users' express agreement. Fears of financial fraud, identity theft, and unlawful surveillance have increased as a result. Furthermore, the frequency and sophistication of data breaches and cyberattacks have increased, exposing private data to nefarious individuals. In addition to hurting people, these instances undermine confidence in businesses and the larger digital economy.

Global governments and regulatory organizations have passed extensive data protection laws in response to these data privacy concerns. The General Data Protection Regulation (GDPR) of the European Union is one of the most prominent frameworks, having gone into effect in 2018. To offer people more control over their information, GDPR imposes strict guidelines on the gathering, using, and retaining of personal data. Important clauses include the need to obtain an individual's express consent before collecting personal data, the right of individuals to access and correct their data, and the need for enterprises to report data breaches to authorities within 72 hours.

Significant penalties for non-compliance with GDPR are also in place; they can amount to as much as 4% of a company's yearly worldwide revenue. This legal framework has raised the bar for data privacy, influencing laws in other jurisdictions and encouraging businesses worldwide to improve their data security procedures.

The laws governing data privacy are more dispersed in the United States, where there are distinct federal and state legislation. One of the most extensive state-level privacy regulations was passed in 2018, known as the California Consumer Privacy Act (CCPA). Residents of California have rights under the CCPA to access and erase their data, as well as information on what personal data is being collected about them and to whom it is being sold. To allow customers to refuse data sales, the act requires firms to place a "Do Not Sell My Personal Information" link on their websites. Similar privacy laws have been passed by other states, including Virginia and Colorado, indicating an increasing trend toward stronger data protection regulations in the US.

In addition to the CCPA and GDPR, there are many additional international rules, each with its requirements. For example, the Personal Data Protection Bill in India, the General Data Protection Law (LGPD) in Brazil, and the Act on the Protection of Personal Information (APPI) in Japan are all intended to safeguard personal data and guarantee that companies manage it appropriately. Common themes throughout these regulations include the necessity of responsibility, openness, and the defense of individual rights. However, they also consider the cultural and legal settings unique to the area, which results in differences in the rules and procedures for enforcing them.

Organizations need help adhering to these regulatory obligations. First, it can take time to comprehend and apply the many changing requirements, especially for international corporations with operations in several different countries. Significant resources are needed to ensure compliance, including solid data management systems, legal knowledge, and continuous monitoring and auditing procedures. Organizations must also balance operational effectiveness, innovation, and regulatory compliance. Strict data privacy laws occasionally impede data-driven business models, forcing organizations to modify procedures and create fresh approaches to harness data while upholding individuals' privacy rights.

Additionally, adhering to regulations involves more than just avoiding penalties and legal ramifications. It also consists in establishing and preserving trust among stakeholders and customers. Being a proponent of data privacy might provide you with a competitive edge at a time when privacy infractions and data breaches make headline news. Customers are more inclined to interact with businesses that prioritize protecting their personal information as they become more conscious of their rights around privacy. Building this trust requires being open and honest about data practices, communicating privacy policies clearly and concisely, and responding quickly to data events.

In addition to adhering to regulations, firms must implement best practices around data security and privacy. This entails implementing robust encryption techniques to safeguard data, conducting frequent security audits to find and fix weaknesses, and offering training courses to staff members to inform them of the best data privacy practices and guidelines. Another crucial technique is data reduction, gathering only the information required for particular goals and keeping it as long as necessary. Organizations can improve personal data protection, lower the risk of breaches, and guarantee regulatory compliance by implementing these procedures.

In conclusion, the digital landscape is heavily influenced by data privacy issues and regulatory constraints, which reflects the growing significance of safeguarding personal data in an increasingly interconnected world. Strong data privacy safeguards, adherence to laws like the CCPA and GDPR, and consumer trust are all necessary to protect sensitive data, prevent adverse legal and financial outcomes, and preserve consumer confidence. The dedication to data privacy will continue to be crucial to ethical and sustainable business practices as technology develops and data gains value. Organizations need to manage the complicated legal landscape to prosper in the digital age, put best practices into place, and promote a privacy-conscious culture.

CHAPTER VII

Technological Barriers and Integration

Challenges in integrating new technologies

Organizations in various industries confront a complex problem when it comes to integrating new technology into their current systems. Although adopting new technologies is driven by the promise of innovation, efficiency, and competitive advantage, the integration process frequently faces considerable obstacles. Technical complexity, organizational inertia, legal limitations, and the requirement for cultural adaptation are the leading causes of these difficulties. These obstacles must be recognized and overcome to integrate technology successfully.

The technical complexity of incorporating new technology is one of the main obstacles. Artificial intelligence, blockchain, and cloud computing are examples of modern technologies that are frequently complex and need specialized skills to be used well. Many times, especially in well-established firms, existing systems are constructed on legacy infrastructure that is difficult to integrate with modern technologies. Due to this incompatibility, significant customization is required, which can be expensive and time-consuming. Large-scale data migrations, integrity checks, and system security maintenance are other possible integration tasks that need careful design and execution. Organizations may find it challenging to handle these complexities with sufficient technological know-how and resources, which could result in delays, higher expenses, and even failures.

Another critical obstacle to the incorporation of technology is organizational inertia. Well-established companies frequently have ingrained, resistant-to-change procedures, structures, and cultures. Workers used to current processes could be hesitant to embrace new ones out of concern about job loss, interruption, or a challenging learning curve. Effective change management techniques, such as thorough training programs, support systems to facilitate the transition, and clear communication about the advantages of the new technology, are needed to overcome this resistance. Establishing a culture of innovation and flexibility is crucial for leadership, as it guarantees that staff members are interested and driven to adopt novel technologies. The potential of even the most sophisticated technologies may be thwarted if organizational inertia is not addressed.

Regulatory restrictions also pose significant obstacles to the integration of new technology. Numerous sectors are highly regulated, especially those that deal with financial services, healthcare, and telecommunications. Although these laws aim to safeguard consumers, uphold equity, and preserve market stability, they may also impede the rate at which new technologies are adopted. Adherence to regulatory mandates frequently necessitates copious documentation, meticulous examination, and, occasionally, adjustments to the technology itself. The GDPR, for example, mandates that businesses put strict data protection procedures in place. Integrating data-intensive technologies like big data analytics and artificial intelligence might make it more challenging. To maintain compliance without limiting innovation, navigating the regulatory landscape necessitates a thorough understanding of the pertinent legislation and proactive contact with authorities.

Another crucial component of adopting new technologies is cultural adaptation. Implementing cutting-edge technologies frequently calls for a change in corporate culture that emphasizes cooperation, constant learning, and openness to change. It could be necessary for traditional hierarchical structures to change to facilitate more flexible, cross-functional teams that can react swiftly to technological advances. Innovation must be promoted by promoting an experimental culture where workers can make and grow from mistakes. In addition, a diverse workforce fosters innovation and problem-solving, making integrating new technologies more accessible. Organizations that want to guarantee that their staff is ready to adopt and use the latest technology efficiently must invest in cultural change programs.

Financial limitations may also make it more challenging to integrate new technologies. While novel technology can bring significant long-term benefits, the initial investment required for acquisition, deployment, and training can be enormous. Tiny and medium-sized businesses (SMEs) may need helping to set aside the necessary funds for these kinds of expenditures. Even larger firms must ensure that the return on investment outweighs the costs by carefully weighing the pros and cons. Financial limitations may cause innovations to be adopted piecemeal, which could restrict their efficacy since they are applied gradually rather than all at once. Overcoming this obstacle requires securing sufficient funding, which can be obtained through government grants, external investments, or internal budgets.

Furthermore, integrating new technologies is significantly hampered by cybersecurity concerns. Organizations are more susceptible to cyberattacks when implementing increasingly sophisticated and networked technologies. Strong cybersecurity safeguards must be in place during integration to preserve operational integrity and safeguard sensitive data. This entails raising the staff's understanding of cybersecurity issues and implementing technical measures like encryption and access limits. A thorough cybersecurity strategy must include incident response planning, ongoing monitoring, and regular security evaluations. The benefits of technology integration can be undermined by failing to address cybersecurity concerns, which can result in data breaches, financial losses, and reputational damage.

In summary, incorporating new technology into legacy systems is a complex process that requires carefully considering organizational, financial, cultural, legal, managerial, and cybersecurity considerations. Organizations must overcome these obstacles through strategic planning, efficient change management, and a dedication to ongoing learning and adaptation. Organizations may fully utilize new technologies and drive innovation, efficiency, and competitive advantage in an increasingly digital world by taking proactive measures to overcome these difficulties. Organizations that successfully integrate technology are better positioned to prosper in the dynamic and quickly changing technological landscape and improve their operating capabilities.

Legacy systems and their limitations

Older computer systems, software, or apps that have been used for a long time are known as legacy systems, sometimes known as "legacy software" or "heritage systems." Even though these methods may have worked effectively for businesses in the past, they can provide severe constraints and issues in today's quickly changing technology landscape.

One of legacy systems' main drawbacks is their antiquated technological architecture. Many legacy systems were created using hardware, architectures, and programming languages that have been used for a while. These systems consequently need more adaptability, scalability, and interoperability to satisfy the requirements of contemporary business contexts. The complexity and cost of upgrading or expanding the functionality of legacy systems can be unnecessarily high because compatibility problems and workarounds must be navigated. It can be challenging to locate competent developers who are conversant with older technologies, which exacerbates the issue.

Furthermore, outdated systems frequently need more reliable performance. Patchwork fixes, adaptations, and revisions over many years can result in a complex network of code that is challenging to manage and troubleshoot. Consequently, outdated systems could have frequent outages, sluggish reaction times, and heightened vulnerability to mistakes and malfunctions. These performance problems can impair consumer satisfaction, interfere with business operations, and limit productivity. Moreover, companies may face security flaws and compliance issues if vendors no longer maintain obsolete hardware and software components.

Another critical drawback is the incapacity of legacy systems to adapt to changing business requirements and technology breakthroughs. Organizations must be flexible and sensitive to shifting market conditions, customer demands, and regulatory requirements in today's fast-paced digital economy. Legacy systems struggle to adjust to these changing demands because of their inflexible architectures and monolithic designs. It can take a lot of effort and time to integrate new features, scale to meet demand or integrate with contemporary apps. This rigidity can hamper an organization's potential to prosper in the digital era by impeding innovation and competitive differentiation.

Moreover, sophisticated data analytics and reporting capabilities should be present in legacy systems. Organizations need quick access to accurate and actionable insights to drive strategic goals and enhance performance in an era where data-driven decision-making is critical. Modern businesses want real-time visibility and analytics capabilities, which legacy systems fail to deliver due to their restricted data processing capabilities and fragmented architectures. Decision-making procedures may be delayed and rendered inaccurate by the laborious and prone-to-error process of extracting, transforming, and evaluating data from many sources.

Legacy systems also present severe difficulties for risk management and regulatory compliance. Given the growing incidence of data privacy rules, cybersecurity concerns, and industry standards, organizations must ensure that their systems comply with strict compliance requirements. Due to their antiquated security procedures and deficiency of integrated compliance tools, legacy systems may not meet these requirements, putting businesses at risk of fines from authorities, legal ramifications, and harm to their brand. To further compound the danger, legacy systems' intrinsic complexity, and brittleness can make them easy targets for cyberattacks and data breaches.

To sum up, legacy systems have a lot of drawbacks and difficulties that might impede an organization's ability to innovate, expand, and compete. These systems pose a serious obstacle to digital transition because of their antiquated technological infrastructure, subpar performance and dependability, rigidity, constrained analytical capabilities, and compliance issues. However, because of worries about expense, disruption, and risk, many firms still rely on legacy systems despite these difficulties. Using strategies including system replacement, integration, migration, and steady evolution, companies must create a roadmap for legacy modernization to overcome these constraints and realize the full potential of digital technology. Organizations should position themselves for success in the digital age by proactively addressing the limits of legacy systems, which will foster creativity, agility, and long-term growth.

Strategies for successful technology adoption

Technology adoption fosters creativity, productivity, and competitiveness in today's ever-changing corporate environment. For technology adoption to be effective, organizations must take a strategic approach, whether embracing emerging technologies, upgrading infrastructure, or implementing new applications. By implementing a few critical techniques, organizations may maximize the return on their investments and manage the challenges of adopting new technologies.

First and foremost, companies must ensure that technology supports their commercial and strategic goals. It's crucial to evaluate current capabilities comprehensively, pinpoint areas needing development, and establish precise goals for technology adoption before investing in new technologies. Organizations can make sure that investments are made in projects that will yield the most significant commercial value by coordinating technological initiatives with strategic priorities. Additionally, firms can effectively allocate resources, prioritize activities, and gauge progress using predetermined measures when they have a clear vision and roadmap for adopting technology.

Second, firms must involve essential stakeholders during the technology adoption process. The use of technology necessitates the support and buy-in of crucial stakeholders, including customers, employees, and executives. Leaders must explain the reasoning behind technology initiatives, highlight the advantages for relevant parties, and tackle any apprehensions or opposition to modification. Engaging stakeholders at the outset of the process enables firms to obtain significant insights, recognize possible obstacles, and establish agreement over technology adoption tactics.

Furthermore, encouraging a culture of empowerment and cooperation pushes stakeholders to take charge of technology projects, increasing commitment to success and accountability.

Companies also need to make training and development investments to guarantee that staff members possess the abilities and know-how necessary to utilize emerging technology successfully. Workflows, procedures, and job duties are frequently altered due to technology adoption, which can be disruptive without sufficient training and assistance. Offering thorough training courses, workshops, and tools helps staff members acquire the skills necessary to confidently and efficiently use new technologies. Furthermore, companies should encourage a culture of ongoing experimentation and learning by pushing staff members to investigate novel technology, exchange best practices, and work together to develop creative solutions. Organizations can achieve sustained growth and optimize their technological investments by allocating resources toward staff development.

Furthermore, enterprises need to consider user experience and usability when choosing and adopting new technologies. End users' adoption and acceptance of new technologies are contingent upon several aspects, including but not limited to user-friendly interfaces, intuitive workflows, and seamless integration with existing systems. Organizations must include end users in selecting technology, obtain feedback on user requirements and preferences, and conduct usability testing to detect and resolve any usability problems. Additionally, minimizing resistance to change and facilitating smooth transitions are made possible by continuing to support and assist end users throughout the technology adoption process. Organizations may boost user happiness, productivity, and efficiency by putting the user experience first, leading to increased adoption and success.

Enterprises must embrace an agile and iterative methodology when implementing technology, facilitating flexibility, experimentation, and adaptability to evolving needs and situations. There are delays, cost overruns, and mismatches between technological solutions and business needs due to the rigid and inflexible nature of traditional waterfall approaches to technology adoption. Organizations can break down large projects into smaller, more manageable tasks, deliver value incrementally, and react fast to changes in priorities and feedback by using agile approaches like Scrum and Kanban. Organizations can reduce risks, expedite time-to-market, and improve the delivery of technology solutions by adopting agile principles.

A strategic, all-encompassing approach that includes user experience, agility, stakeholder engagement, staff development, and alignment with corporate objectives is necessary for effective technology adoption. Using these techniques, firms may effectively negotiate the intricacies of technology adoption, surmount obstacles, and fully leverage their technological investments. Successful technology adoption ultimately involves more than just putting new systems or tools in place; it also entails motivating staff members, bringing about significant change, and producing measurable business results that advance companies in an increasingly digital environment.

CHAPTER VIII

Market and Consumer Trust

Building consumer trust in Fintech

Establishing consumer trust is critical to the success of fintech businesses in the fast-paced, cutthroat industry of today. Fintech, an acronym for financial technology, refers to a broad category of creative approaches that use technology to deliver financial services. These approaches include peer-to-peer lending, robo-advisors, digital payments, and blockchain-based transactions. However, establishing and preserving customer trust in fintech is severely hampered by the intrinsic sensitivity of financial transactions and the pervasiveness of cybersecurity risks.

In the fintech sector, transparency is fundamental for fostering customer trust. Customers anticipate being informed straightforwardly and truthfully about the goods and services provided and any relevant terms and conditions. Fintech companies must offer thorough information on fees, charges, risks, and privacy policies to enable customers to make knowledgeable decisions about their financial transactions. Transparency also applies to data handling procedures, as customers' concerns about the collection, usage, and security of their economic and personal data are growing. As a result, fintech businesses must show that they are committed to protecting customer data and upholding privacy rights by being open and honest about their data privacy and security policies.

Another critical component in increasing customer confidence in fintech is security. Given the increase in data breaches and cyberattacks, customers are understandably worried about the security of their financial information while using fintech services. Robust cybersecurity procedures must be put in place by fintech businesses to guard against fraud, illegal access, and data breaches. Encryption, multi-factor authentication, safe data storage, frequent security audits, and incident response procedures are all part of this. Fintech companies may boost consumer confidence and reassure them that their financial transactions are safe and secure by emphasizing security and proactively reducing cyber dangers.

Performance and dependability are crucial elements of customer confidence in FinTech. Customers anticipate having uninterrupted access to fintech services anytime they need them. Fintech enterprises must allocate resources towards robust infrastructure, duplicate systems, and capacities for catastrophe recovery to guarantee elevated accessibility and dependability of their offerings. Fintech businesses must also provide reliable performance, quick reaction times, low latency, and seamless user experiences across platforms and devices. By offering dependable and high-performing services, fintech businesses may stand out from rivals in the industry and gain customers' trust.

Building consumer trust in fintech also requires providing excellent customer care and assistance. As the world grows more digital, customers want prompt, individualized assistance when encountering problems or inquiries about fintech products. To promptly help and resolve client inquiries, fintech organizations must allocate resources toward customer service channels, including chatbots, email, phone support, and social media. Additionally, proactive communication regarding new features, upgrades, and changes to the service keeps users informed and involved. Fintech businesses can cultivate a good rapport with customers and gradually increase their loyalty by prioritizing customer care and assistance.

Another essential component of consumer confidence in fintech is regulatory compliance. Consumers expect fintech companies to abide by all applicable laws, regulations, and industry standards to safeguard their interests and guarantee ethical and transparent business processes. Fintech companies must stay current on regulatory changes, comply with data protection and anti-money laundering (AML) laws, know their customers (KYC), and undertake audits and assessments regularly to ensure compliance. By showcasing their dedication to regulatory compliance, fintech companies may give consumers peace of mind that their financial transactions are safe, lawful, and moral.

Finally, a brand's integrity and reputation influence consumer trust in fintech. Customers are more inclined to believe in well-known, established businesses with a reputation for providing high-quality goods and services. Fintech businesses need to invest in enhancing their reputation as a brand through satisfying client experiences, open communication, and moral business conduct. Additionally, fintech companies can establish their legitimacy and improve their credibility in the eyes of consumers by forming collaborations with reputable financial institutions, industry associations, and regulatory bodies. Fintech businesses may gain customers' trust and set themselves up for long-term success in the market by building a solid reputation and brand credibility.

To sum up, fintech startups must develop consumer trust to thrive in the cutthroat financial services sector. Fintech companies may establish robust customer relationships and stand out in the market by prioritizing transparency, security, reliability, customer service, regulatory compliance, reputation, and brand credibility. Ultimately, consumer trust is the cornerstone of a successful fintech company, allowing them to draw in new clients, encourage the uptake of their goods and services, and experience long-term growth in the digital economy.

Addressing market skepticism

As with any industry, businesses participating in fintech, which is seeing tremendous technical improvements, must address market distrust. Several things, such as doubts about the durability of business models, ambiguity around regulatory compliance, and worries about the dependability of new technology, can cause market skepticism. In the fintech sector, where technological advancements are causing substantial upheavals in conventional financial services, winning over customers, investors, and other stakeholders requires resolving market mistrust.

Setting open communication and transparency as top priorities will help fintech overcome market distrust. Fintech businesses need to be open and honest with their customers, investors, and authorities about their goods, services, and business procedures. Fintech companies may control expectations and establish credibility with stakeholders by being transparent about the risks and limitations of their offerings. Furthermore, by encouraging open lines of communication, fintech businesses may proactively address issues and comments, showcasing their dedication to responsibility and ongoing development.

Setting security and compliance as top priorities is another strategy for dealing with market distrust. Given the delicate nature of financial transactions, customers and investors are naturally worried about the security of fintech platforms and preserving their economic and personal data. Fintech companies must invest in solid cybersecurity safeguards, compliance programs, and risk management procedures to reduce security risks and guarantee regulatory compliance. Fintech companies may ease worries about fraud, data breaches, and regulatory scrutiny by showcasing their dedication to security and compliance. This helps them gain the trust of investors, consumers, and regulators.

Furthermore, addressing market mistrust can benefit fintech organizations by establishing a track record of success and dependability. Fintech companies may build their credibility and trustworthiness by fulfilling performance targets, providing high-quality products and services, and generating favorable results for investors and customers. This could entail using case studies, industry credentials, and client endorsements to highlight accomplishments and convey value. Furthermore, forming strategic alliances with well-known financial institutions, technology suppliers, and government agencies can help fintech startups gain legitimacy and credibility in the eyes of stakeholders.

Additionally, educating the market about the advantages and potential of fintech can address skepticism and promote acceptance of new technology. Fintech concepts may be foreign to many investors and customers, and their applicability and efficacy may be questioned. Fintech companies may proactively educate the market through content marketing, public outreach, and thought leadership. Fintech companies may demystify the technology and inspire confidence in its capabilities by outlining how fintech solutions operate, emphasizing their advantages over traditional financial services, and offering concrete examples of successful applications.

Fintech companies can overcome regulatory obstacles and market distrust by aggressively interacting with industry associations and regulators. Fintech companies, especially those in highly regulated industries like payments and banking, are concerned about regulatory unpredictability and compliance needs. Fintech companies can influence the regulatory landscape and cultivate stakeholder confidence through partnerships with regulators, active participation in industry forums, and advocacy for transparent and encouraging regulatory frameworks. Fintech companies can also ensure that their goods and services adhere to industry norms and regulatory regulations by consulting with legal and compliance specialists.

In conclusion, fintech businesses that want to succeed and establish a reputation in the cutthroat financial services sector must confront market skepticism. Fintech businesses may assuage fears and foster confidence with customers, investors, and regulators by prioritizing transparency, security, dependability, education, and regulatory engagement. Ultimately, dealing with market skepticism necessitates a multidimensional strategy that includes stakeholder participation, risk management, communication, and credibility building. Fintech businesses can set themselves up for success and encourage the market's broad acceptance of their goods and services by proactively addressing skeptics.

The role of transparency and education

For example, transparency and education are essential in the corporate, government, and technological spheres of modern civilization. Transparency and education are necessary in fintech since they promote adoption, trust, and innovation in the financial services sector. While education entails disseminating information on fintech principles, advantages, hazards, and best practices, transparency refers to freely sharing information about goods, services, procedures, and results. To reduce risks, make educated decisions, and engage productively in the fintech ecosystem, stakeholders such as investors, regulators, and consumers can all benefit from increased openness and education.

Gaining the trust and confidence of investors and customers is one of the primary purposes of transparency in the fintech industry. Giving precise and understandable information on the characteristics, advantages, dangers, and expenses of fintech goods and services is critical to transparency. Fintech companies may build credibility and ease worries about dependability and trustworthiness by being open and honest about how their solutions operate, how they're governed, and how they safeguard customer data and privacy. Furthermore, openness promotes responsibility and accountability among fintech companies, resulting in moral behavior and just treatment of clients.

Education plays a complementary role in the fintech industry by equipping stakeholders with knowledge and comprehension of fintech concepts, technologies, and applications. Fintech may be unknown to many investors and consumers, and many may need clarification on its applicability or efficacy. Fintech firms, trade groups, and academic institutions may help stakeholders understand fintech and make well-informed decisions regarding its acceptance and use by offering educational tools like articles, manuals, tutorials, webinars, and seminars. Additionally, education allows investors and customers to recognize possible dangers and advantages related to fintech, enabling them to negotiate the quickly changing environment successfully.

In underprivileged communities, transparency and education also greatly aid financial inclusion and literacy. Fintech can democratize financial services accessibility by making it easier and more affordable for people and companies to obtain banking, payments, lending, investing, and insurance services. But to truly achieve financial inclusion, hurdles must be removed, including a lack of knowledge, confidence, and comprehension of fintech solutions. Fintech companies have the potential to enable underprivileged communities to engage in the digital economy, generate wealth, and enhance their financial well-being by advocating for transparency and offering customized education that caters to the requirements of varied populations.

Furthermore, tackling regulatory obstacles and encouraging cooperation between fintech businesses and regulators depend heavily on transparency and education. Regulatory compliance is a significant worry for fintech companies, especially those in highly regulated industries like banking, payments, and securities. Fintech companies may show regulators they are committed to regulatory compliance and gain their trust by being open and honest about their operations, procedures, and compliance initiatives. Furthermore, by filling knowledge gaps and promoting productive discourse on regulatory matters, education programs targeted at regulators can eventually result in more receptive and accommodating regulatory frameworks for fintech innovation.

To sum up, openness and learning are essential foundations of a healthy fintech industry. Fintech companies have the potential to enhance confidence, encourage adoption, promote financial inclusion, address regulatory obstacles, and stimulate innovation in the financial services sector using transparency and education. Transparency and education also enable regulators, investors, consumers, and other stakeholders to actively participate in the fintech revolution, reduce risks, and make well-informed decisions. As fintech transforms the financial landscape, transparency and education will continue to be crucial facilitators of development, prosperity, and fair access to financial

CHAPTER IX

Financial Inclusion

The role of Fintech in promoting financial inclusion

To promote social inclusion, lower poverty, and promote economic progress, all individuals and enterprises must have access to and utilize adequate and inexpensive financial services. This is known as financial inclusion. Millions of people are still underserved or left out of the official financial system globally due to remote locations, high transaction fees, and restricted access to traditional banking services. Fintech, or financial technology, has become a potent force in promoting financial inclusion by utilizing technology to overcome these obstacles and increase underprivileged populations' access to financial services.

Fintech facilitates financial inclusion primarily by making essential banking services accessible via digital means. Many people in underprivileged regions do not have access to physical bank branches or ATMs because of infrastructure constraints or remote locations. Fintech businesses provide digital banking solutions that let people use their smartphones or other internet-enabled devices to effortlessly and securely access financial services. Examples of these solutions include digital wallets, online account opening, and mobile banking apps. For those lacking or limited access to traditional bank accounts, these digital channels offer a lifeline by enabling them to perform fundamental financial operations like deposits, withdrawals, payments, and transfers.

Furthermore, through creative lending and microfinance solutions, fintech helps underprivileged communities access credit and savings opportunities. Conventional banks frequently use credit scoring methods based on collateral and credit history, which excludes many people with little to no credit history. Fintech companies evaluate creditworthiness and extend loans to those who would not be considered acceptable by traditional lenders by utilizing alternative data sources, such as transaction history, social media activity, and mobile phone usage statistics. Fintech companies also provide digital platforms for investing and saving, enabling people to save, invest, and accumulate wealth at a minimal cost, even with small sums of money.

Fintech is also essential in helping underprivileged groups have greater access to risk management and insurance options. Disadvantaged communities are home to many people and companies that are susceptible to various dangers, such as agricultural failures, medical issues, and natural disasters, all of which can have catastrophic financial repercussions. Fintech businesses provide cutting-edge insurance solutions that are affordable and suited to the needs of marginalized communities, like microinsurance and parametric insurance. Fintech businesses can offer insurance solutions that are cost-effective, easily accessible, and tailored to the unique risks encountered by marginalized communities. This allows them to foster resilience and financial security through technology, data analytics, and digital distribution channels.

Fintech also encourages financial awareness and education, which allows people in marginalized groups to make better financial decisions and enhance their financial well-being. Due to their lack of fundamental financial literacy, many members of underprivileged groups are susceptible to fraud, exploitation, and poor financial resource management. Fintech businesses provide educational resources to assist people grasp concepts like debt management, investing, saving, and budgeting. These resources include interactive apps, classes on financial literacy, and individualized financial advice. Fintech enables people to take charge of their money, make wise decisions, and reach their financial objectives by advancing financial literacy and education.

Fintech also promotes economic empowerment and entrepreneurship by giving underrepresented small firms and entrepreneurs access to money, markets, and resources. Traditional banks frequently have strict qualifying requirements for company loans and demand collateral, which prevents many entrepreneurs from obtaining funding. Fintech companies facilitate the connection between underprivileged entrepreneurs and investors eager to support their business initiatives through peer-to-peer lending networks, crowdfunding platforms, and alternative financing platforms. Fintech companies also provide e-commerce platforms, digital marketplaces, and payment solutions that help small businesses grow their client base, penetrate new markets, and compete more successfully in the digital economy.

To sum up, fintech is essential to advancing financial inclusion because it uses technology to lower obstacles to access and increase the number of acceptable and reasonably priced financial services available to disadvantaged communities. Fintech enables people and businesses in underprivileged communities to engage in the formal financial system, develop resilience, and enhance their financial well-being. It provides digital banking, credit solutions, insurance, and financial education. Fintech can significantly improve millions of lives globally by fostering financial inclusion and driving good social and economic impact as long as it keeps innovating and evolving.

Case studies of successful inclusion initiatives

Case studies of prosperous inclusion efforts offer essential insights into the effects and efficacy of different tactics and methods of financial inclusion promotion. These programs show how fintech companies work with government agencies, non-profits, and other stakeholders to meet the unique demands and difficulties faced by underrepresented groups, such as women, low-income people, people living in rural areas, and small enterprises. Through an analysis of these case studies, we can pinpoint critical success elements, optimal methodologies, and insights gained that can guide forthcoming endeavors to advance financial inclusion worldwide.

The M-Pesa mobile money platform in Kenya is a noteworthy case study, as it has revolutionized the financial sector and enabled millions of individuals to access banking services reasonably. M-Pesa, the leading mobile network provider in Kenya, was introduced in 2007 by Safaricom. With the help of their phones, customers may pay their bills, make deposits and withdrawals, and access other financial services. The platform uses Kenya's robust telecommunications infrastructure and high rate of mobile phone adoption to offer accessible financial services to people living in both urban and rural locations. With over 40 million registered users and over half of Kenya's GDP processed through the platform yearly, M-Pesa has vastly improved financial access and inclusion in the country.

Another striking case study is the Grameen Bank microfinance program in Bangladesh, which popularized microcredit and enabled millions of women to escape poverty through business. Nobel laureate Muhammad Yunus founded Grameen Bank in 1976 to give small loans to underprivileged people, especially women so that they could launch or grow small companies. With borrowers organizing into groups to assist one another and repay loans collectively, the bank functions on the tenets of trust, solidarity, and social collateral. In Bangladesh and other nations worldwide, Grameen Bank's creative microfinance strategy has shown to be incredibly successful in advancing financial inclusion, economic empowerment, and social development.

Additionally, the Aadhaar biometric identity system implemented by the Indian government has been essential in advancing financial inclusion and increasing the number of unbanked people in India with access to banking services. Since its launch in 2009, Aadhaar has provided every resident of India with a unique 12-digit identification number that is connected to their biometric and demographic information. Through biometric scanners and the Aadhaar system, people can swiftly and securely validate their identity, making it easier for banks and other financial institutions to process account openings and transactions. Know Your Customer (KYC) procedures have been streamlined, identity fraud has decreased, and economic access for India's underprivileged communities has increased because of UID.

In addition, the Kiva microlending network also offers a powerful illustration of how technology may facilitate global connections between lenders and borrowers toto advance financial inclusion and reduce poverty. Kiva, established in 2005, enables people to lend modest sums of money to company owners and startups in marginalized areas worldwide. The money is borrowed, and borrowers use it for emergency costs, education, and business startup or expansion. Through the use of social media and technology, Kiva's peer-to-peer lending strategy democratizes access to cash and encourages economic empowerment at the local level.

Finally, case examples of practical inclusion efforts show how fintech and creative thinking can promote financial inclusion and empower marginalized communities worldwide. These initiatives—from peer-to-peer lending and mobile money platforms to microfinance organizations and biometric identification systems—illustrate how technology, entrepreneurship, and teamwork can spur beneficial social and economic change. Examining these case studies, policymakers, practitioners, and stakeholders can gain essential insights and lessons. These can help guide future initiatives to advance financial inclusion and build a more fair and inclusive financial system for all.

Future prospects for financial inclusion

Financial inclusion has bright future possibilities thanks to developing business models, new technology, and changing regulatory environments. Financial inclusion projects are anticipated to increase the number of unbanked and underbanked people and enterprises worldwide with access to banking services, credit, insurance, and savings opportunities as the world economy grows more digital and interconnected. Future financial inclusion is shaped by several significant trends and developments propelling the economic system's evolution toward greater accessibility and inclusivity.

The ongoing development of digital financial services is one of the key themes influencing financial inclusion in the future. The delivery of financial services has been entirely transformed by mobile technology, internet connectivity, and digital payment platforms. People can now quickly and economically access banking services through smartphones or other internet-enabled devices. In underserved and distant locations where traditional banking infrastructure is inadequate or nonexistent, digital banking solutions like digital wallets, online account opening, and mobile banking apps are progressively replacing conventional banking infrastructure as the primary means of obtaining banking services.

Furthermore, the financial services sector is seeing unprecedented innovation and disruption due to the emergence of fintech firms and creative business models, opening up new avenues for promoting financial inclusion. Fintech companies are increasing underprivileged people's access to credit and savings options by utilizing technology, data analytics, and alternative credit scoring algorithms. By eliminating traditional banks and other financial intermediaries, peer-to-peer lending platforms, crowdfunding websites, and digital microfinance organizations bring lenders and borrowers together directly, democratizing access to cash for individuals and small enterprises.

In addition, government-driven programs and regulatory changes are essential in advancing financial inclusion and increasing underprivileged groups' access to banking services. Around the world, many governments are putting laws and rules into place to safeguard consumers, stimulate digital financial services, and foster competition and innovation in the financial industry. Digital identity systems, like Huduma Namba in Kenya and Aadhaar in India, are making it easier for people to use banking services by giving them safe and reliable ways to prove who they are, expediting Know Your Customer (KYC) procedures, and lowering identity theft.

Furthermore, cooperative initiatives to advance financial inclusion and address the particular needs of marginalized groups are being fueled by collaborations between governments, financial institutions, fintech firms, and non-profit organizations. Industry coalitions, public-private partnerships, and multilateral efforts combine their resources, knowledge, and networks to create novel ideas, test out fresh strategies, and expand effective financial inclusion measures. By utilizing the combined abilities and assets of various stakeholders, these collaborations are expediting the process of attaining universal financial services accessibility and promoting sustainable development and economic expansion.

Additionally, as the informal economy continues to be formalized and digitalized, new avenues for advancing financial inclusion and extending access to banking services for people and companies in the informal sector are opening up. Digital payment platforms, e-commerce marketplaces, and online marketplaces facilitate financial transactions to reduce dependency on cash and unofficial financial channels. They allow people to access banking services, receive payments, and do business digitally. In addition, incorporating digital financial services into government social protection initiatives, such as subsidies and cash transfers, encourages financial inclusion and offers a safety net to disadvantaged groups.

In conclusion, technological advancement, legislative changes, and cooperative alliances will all contribute to the promising future of financial inclusion. Millions of unbanked and underbanked people and businesses are expected to gain access to banking services, credit, insurance, and savings opportunities as digital financial services become more widely available, reasonably priced, and easily accessed. This will open up new avenues for prosperity and economic empowerment. To create a monetary system that is more equitable and inclusive for all, players from the public and commercial sectors should prioritize inclusion, embrace innovation, and collaborate.

CHAPTER X

Personalized Financial Services

The trend towards personalized financial products

The trend toward personalized financial services has significantly changed how financial products and services are created, advertised, and provided to customers. Rather than taking a one-size-fits-all strategy, personalization entails adjusting financial products to each consumer's specific needs, tastes, and circumstances. Technological developments, data analytics, and customer segmentation strategies are driving this trend because they allow financial institutions to collect and analyze enormous volumes of data about their customers' financial behavior, tastes, and life phases. Financial institutions can use this data to provide tailored financial experiences and products that offer customers more value, relevance, and engagement.

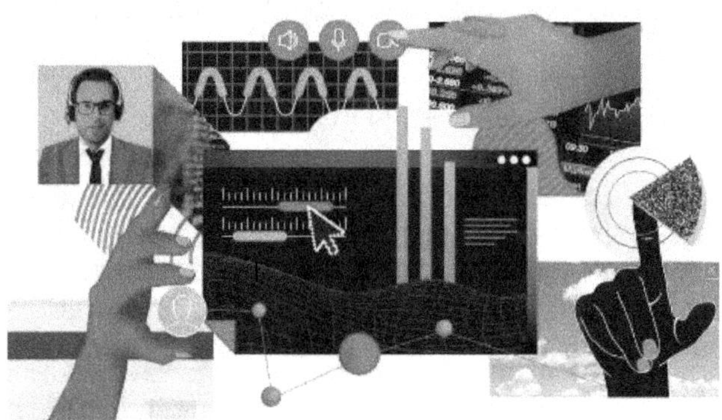

The increasing requirement for specialized solutions that cater to customers' unique demands and preferences is one of the main factors driving the trend toward personalized financial services. Consumers nowadays have a wide range of financial objectives, lifestyles, and risk tolerances. They also anticipate that financial services and products will be tailored to their unique needs and goals. Financial institutions may provide services and solutions that are more suited to the needs and ambitions of their customers thanks to personalization, whether those needs are managing debt, supporting education, saving for retirement, or purchasing a home. Financial institutions can improve client happiness, loyalty, and retention, fostering long-term relationships and profitability by customizing financial services to each customer's needs.

Furthermore, financial institutions can now collect and analyze a multitude of consumer data, including transaction history, spending patterns, income levels, credit ratings, and life events, thanks to technology and data analytics developments. Financial institutions can offer personalized suggestions, products, and services in real time by utilizing artificial intelligence, machine learning, and predictive analytics to gain insights into their customers' financial behavior, preferences, and needs. For instance, based on customers' buying patterns and life events, banks and fintech firms can leverage data analytics to find chances to cross-sell pertinent items like credit cards, loans, and insurance.

Moreover, personalization covers the entire customer journey, from engagement and onboarding to customer care and support, going beyond just product recommendations. Financial institutions can customize marketing messages, communication channels, and user interfaces to each individual's interests and behaviors using data analytics and customer segmentation approaches. For example, based on customers' financial objectives, preferences, and life stages, banks and fintech companies can give tailored offers, reminders, and instructional content through personalized marketing emails, mobile notifications, and in-app communications.

Furthermore, providing customers with timely and pertinent support, personalized customer care, and support experiences—like chatbots, virtual assistants, and self-service portals—can raise customer happiness and engagement.

Personalized financial services are becoming more popular, but this brings up significant issues with data security, privacy, and trust. Financial institutions must ensure robust measures are in place to protect customers' sensitive information and privacy rights as they collect and analyze ever-increasing volumes of consumer data to personalize products and services. This entails putting strong data encryption, access controls, and data anonymization strategies into place to stop unwanted access, security breaches, and improper use of customer data. Financial organizations should also give customers explicit knowledge and control over their data by being open and honest about their data-gathering methods, algorithmic usage, and privacy rules.

Conclusively, the financial industry is dramatically changing toward personalized financial services, propelled by technological breakthroughs, data analytics, and rising consumer expectations. Financial institutions can provide customized solutions that cater to individual customers' distinct requirements and inclinations through personalization, which increases client satisfaction, loyalty, and engagement. Financial institutions can offer tailored experiences, products, and suggestions that improve customer satisfaction and foster long-term relationships by utilizing data analytics and client segmentation approaches. To guarantee that customers' sensitive information is safeguarded, and their rights are upheld, financial institutions must prioritize data privacy, security, and trust as personalization is more common.

How AI and big data are driving personalization

Big data and artificial intelligence (AI) are completely changing how companies interact and comprehend their consumer base, especially regarding customization. Businesses can collect, process, and analyze enormous volumes of data about customer behavior, preferences, and interactions across several channels and touchpoints thanks to artificial intelligence (AI) and big data analytics. Businesses may provide individualized experiences that address each client's particular requirements, interests, and preferences by utilizing AI and big data, which will increase customer satisfaction, loyalty, and engagement.

Predictive analytics and machine learning algorithms are two main ways AI and big data enable personalization. With these technologies, businesses can see correlations, patterns, and trends in customer data, which helps them project customer behavior and preferences for the future. For instance, e-commerce businesses can employ AI algorithms to assess demographic data, browsing patterns, and historical purchase histories to forecast which goods or services a client is likely interested in and provide appropriate product recommendations in real-time. Similarly, banks and other financial organizations can use AI and big data to examine past transactions, credit reports, and spending trends to tailor recommendations for loans, credit cards, and investment opportunities depending on specific individuals' financial objectives and risk profiles.

Additionally, organizations may offer tailored content and messages through various channels and touchpoints, such as websites, mobile applications, social media, email, and advertising platforms, thanks to AI and big data. AI algorithms can tailor website experiences, including product recommendations, offers, and promotions, depending on user preferences and browsing behavior by real-time analysis of consumer data.

Similarly, AI-driven chatbots and virtual assistants can converse naturally with clients, offering tailored support and suggestions in response to their requirements and questions. AI-driven advertising platforms can also send consumers targeted adverts and messages based on their interests, demographics, and online behavior to maximize relevance and efficacy.

Furthermore, by enabling businesses to provide customers with timely and appropriate assistance across numerous channels, AI and significant data drive customization in customer care and support. Artificial intelligence (AI)-driven chatbots and virtual assistants may handle common requests, offer self-service alternatives, and promptly and effectively address problems, freeing human agents to concentrate on more challenging jobs and high-value interactions. AI systems can also evaluate sentiment data and consumer interactions to find areas for improvement and tailor subsequent communications according to the preferences and input of specific individuals. To improve the entire customer experience, banks and other financial institutions, for instance, can utilize AI to evaluate customer support encounters, identify common pain points, and proactively fix concerns.

However, Big data and AI present enormous personalization opportunities, but they also raise critical questions about data security, privacy, and ethics. Businesses must ensure that robust measures are in place to protect customers' sensitive information and privacy rights as they collect and analyze ever-increasing volumes of consumer data to tailor experiences. This entails putting strong data encryption, access controls, and data anonymization strategies into place to stop unwanted access, security breaches, and improper use of customer data. Additionally, companies must give customers explicit knowledge and control over their data by being open and honest about their data-gathering procedures, algorithmic usage, and privacy rules.

In summary, artificial intelligence (AI) and big data facilitate customization by allowing companies to collect, examine, and utilize enormous volumes of customer information to design customized experiences that meet specific requirements and tastes. Artificial intelligence (AI) and big data are revolutionizing how organizations interact with their customers through various channels and touchpoints, from tailored content and messaging to predictive analytics and machine learning algorithms. But as personalization spreads, companies must put ethics, security, and data privacy first to guarantee that customers' rights are upheld, and their private information is safeguarded. Businesses can fully realize the potential of personalization and create remarkable experiences that captivate and delight customers by judiciously utilizing AI and big data.

Examples of personalized Fintech solutions

Personalized fintech solutions, which offer experiences customized to meet each customer's particular wants and preferences, significantly improve the financial services sector. These solutions provide individualized advice, goods, and services in various economic sectors, such as banking, lending, investing, and insurance. They achieve this by utilizing technology, data analytics, and artificial intelligence. Fintech organizations may improve client happiness, loyalty, and engagement through personalization, leading to long-term partnerships and revenue.

Personalized investment platforms, which employ machine learning and algorithms to customize investment recommendations and portfolios based on individual risk profiles, financial goals, and preferences, are one example of a personalized fintech solution. To suggest appropriate investment options, asset allocations, and strategies, these platforms examine variables including age, income, investment horizon, risk tolerance, and investing preferences. Robo-advisors, for instance, employ algorithms to evaluate investors' investment goals and risk tolerance before recommending diverse portfolios of stocks, bonds, and other assets that suit their tastes. Additionally, to assist individuals in more successfully achieving their financial objectives, personalized investment platforms may include features like goal tracking, automated rebalancing, and tax efficiency.

Personalized lending platforms, which evaluate customers' creditworthiness and provide customized loan products and terms using data analytics and machine learning, are another example of a customized fintech service. These systems assess borrowers' risk profiles and establish loan eligibility, interest rates, and repayment conditions by examining variables like credit history, income, employment status, debt-to-income ratio, and spending habits. Peer-to-peer lending systems, for instance, use AI algorithms to match borrowers with private investors who are prepared to fund their loans according to their preferences for risk and return. To accommodate borrowers' unique demands and circumstances, personalized lending platforms may also include features like flexible repayment alternatives, loan customization, and credit monitoring.

Additionally, tailored banking experiences that accommodate unique tastes and lifestyles are provided via personalized banking platforms, which aid customers in better money management. These platforms examine past transactions, spending habits, and financial objectives to give the users individualized recommendations, insights, and services. Budgeting apps, for instance, employ AI algorithms to classify and examine users' spending patterns, spot areas where money can be saved, and offer tailored advice for enhancing financial well-being. Furthermore, real-time alerts, bill payment reminders, and spending insights are just a few services personalized banking platforms may provide to assist customers in managing their money and reaching their financial objectives.

Personalized insurance platforms also provide customized coverage options and insurance products to match individual risk profiles and needs. These platforms evaluate an individual's insurance needs and suggest appropriate coverage options and plans based on an analysis of several characteristics, including insurance history, lifestyle, health, and demographics. Usage-based insurance apps, for instance, track users' driving behaviors and provide customized auto insurance quotes based on variables like mileage, speed, and driving style by utilizing telematics data from linked devices, such as smartphones or cars. To provide customers with a seamless and customized insurance experience, personalized insurance platforms may include features like adjustable coverage limits, policy bundling, and claims support.

In summary, personalized fintech solutions offer tailored experiences that address individual customers' particular requirements and preferences, marking a paradigm shift in the financial services sector. Fintech businesses use technology and data analytics to offer customized suggestions, products, and services across various economic areas. These services include personalized lending solutions, investing platforms, banking apps, and insurance platforms. By leveraging personalization, fintech organizations may improve client satisfaction, loyalty, and engagement, which can lead to long-term connections and profitability in the digital age.

CHAPTER XI

Partnerships and Collaborations

The importance of partnerships in Fintech

In the fintech ecosystem, partnerships and collaborations are essential for promoting innovation, increasing access to financial services, and ensuring long-term success. Fintech businesses frequently work in intricate, highly regulated contexts and deal with client acquisition, regulatory compliance, and operational growth issues. Fintech companies can better address these challenges and accelerate their growth and impact by forming strategic partnerships with other firms, traditional financial institutions, technology providers, regulators, and industry stakeholders. These partnerships allow them to utilize complementary strengths, resources, and expertise.

Accessing complementary skills and resources is one of the main advantages of fintech partnerships. Fintech companies frequently have cutting-edge technology, flexible business plans, and in-depth knowledge of particular financial services sectors, such as lending, wealth management, and payments. However, they might not have the size, distribution networks, and regulatory know-how needed to reach a more extensive client base and negotiate intricate regulatory environments. Fintech businesses can access existing financial institutions' vast client networks, well-known brands, infrastructure, and regulatory compliance frameworks through partnerships, which helps them expand their offerings faster and more effectively. Similarly, traditional financial institutions can get access to cutting-edge technologies, improve client satisfaction, and spur organizational digital transformation by collaborating with fintech firms.

Furthermore, partnerships help fintech companies grow more quickly and affordably by expanding their product offerings and breaking into new industries. Fintech businesses, for instance, might work with other fintech companies, technology suppliers, or established players in the market to incorporate supplementary goods and services—like payment processing, risk management, or user authentication—into their platforms. Fintech companies can better serve their customers' changing demands, stand out from the competition, and improve the value proposition of their offerings by utilizing these collaborations. Furthermore, fintech companies can benefit from relationships with industry groups and regulatory agencies, which can aid in navigating complicated regulatory frameworks, providing access to best practices and market data, and establishing credibility and trust with stakeholders.

Moreover, collaborations facilitate fintech enterprises in meeting the increasing need for seamless and integrated financial solutions across several domains and touchpoints. For instance, customers are coming to expect financial services to be a part of their regular activities, like social networking, travel, and shopping. Fintech companies can offer clients more convenience, choice, and value by directly integrating financial services like loans, insurance, and payments into e-commerce platforms, mobile apps, or partnerships. Fintech organizations can also benefit from leveraging data-driven insights and predictive analytics to tailor products, optimize decision-making, and improve client engagement and retention through collaborations with data providers, analytics firms, and artificial intelligence companies.

Nonetheless, rigorous preparation, interest alignment, and productive teamwork are necessary for fintech partnerships to succeed. Potential partners must be carefully considered by fintech companies based on things like mutual benefit, cultural alignment, strategic fit, and shared goals. In addition, it is imperative that they set up unambiguous governance frameworks, effective communication channels, and performance benchmarks to guarantee that partnerships are mutually advantageous and long-lasting. To reduce risks and ensure collaborations succeed, fintech companies must also handle possible obstacles, including rivalry, conflicts of interest, and regulatory compliance.

In summary, partnerships and collaborations are critical to promoting sustainable growth in the fintech industry, increasing access to financial services, and accelerating innovation. Fintech companies can enhance their ability to address challenges and accelerate their growth and impact by forming strategic partnerships with other firms, traditional financial institutions, technology providers, regulators, and industry stakeholders. These partnerships allow the companies to take advantage of complementary strengths, resources, and expertise. To secure mutual gain and long-term success, however, successful partnerships need rigorous planning, interest alignment, and efficient partner communication. Partnerships will continue to be essential to innovation and expansion in the digital economy as fintech reshapes the financial landscape.

Collaborations between Fintech and traditional financial institutions

In the financial services sector, partnerships between fintech companies and established financial institutions are a prominent trend that promotes innovation, digital transformation, and customer-centricity. Fintech companies frequently have cutting-edge technology, flexible business plans, and in-depth knowledge of particular financial services sectors, such as lending, wealth management, and payments. However, they might need to gain the size, distribution networks, and regulatory know-how required to reach a more extensive client base and negotiate intricate regulatory environments. Traditional financial institutions, on the other hand, may suffer from legacy systems, antiquated procedures, and sluggish innovation cycles while having vast customer networks, well-known brands, infrastructure, and regulatory compliance frameworks. By establishing strategic alliances, these two categories of organizations can take advantage of their complimentary advantages, assets, and knowledge to better tackle these issues and hasten their expansion and influence in the digital era.

Acquiring complementary expertise and resources is one of the main advantages of fintech and traditional financial institutions working together. Partnering with well-established financial institutions can help fintech companies gain access to their vast networks of customers, well-known brands, and distribution channels. To reach a wider audience and expand its capabilities more rapidly and effectively, a fintech company specializing in digital payments, for instance, can collaborate with a bank to offer its payment solutions to its clients. Similarly, by collaborating with fintech companies, traditional financial institutions can access cutting-edge technologies, flexible business structures, and in-depth subject matter knowledge in fields like data analytics, blockchain, and artificial intelligence. This will enable them to accelerate digital transformation and improve customer satisfaction.

Additionally, partnerships between fintech and traditional financial institutions allow both to more quickly and affordably enter new markets and increase the scope of their product offerings. Fintech companies may work with credit unions or banks to provide their cutting-edge goods and services to the bank's current clientele. To offer its loan products to bank consumers, a fintech company specializing in digital lending might collaborate with a bank, taking advantage of its regulatory compliance framework and well-known brand. Furthermore, by forming alliances with fintech companies, established financial institutions can improve the products they offer, set themselves apart from competitors, and better serve the changing needs of their clientele. To draw in and keep tech-savvy clients, a bank might collaborate with a fintech company to provide cutting-edge digital banking services like peer-to-peer payments, mobile wallets, and robo-advisory services.

Moreover, partnerships between fintech and established financial institutions allow both to respond to the increasing need for seamless, integrated financial solutions that cross several touchpoints and domains. Customers are expecting more and more financial services to be a part of their daily lives—whether it be social networking, travel, or shopping. Traditional financial institutions can directly integrate financial services into these experiences through partnerships with fintech companies, offering customers increased choice, convenience, and value. For instance, to provide a smooth payment experience within its mobile banking app, a bank would collaborate with a fintech company specializing in mobile payments. This would allow users to send money to friends and family, divide bills, and easily make purchases.

Nonetheless, cautious preparation, interest alignment, and strong partner collaboration are necessary for fintech and traditional financial institution partnerships to succeed. For mutually beneficial and long-lasting partnerships, both sides must have clear expectations, goals, and governance structures. To reduce risks and guarantee the success of cooperation, they also need to handle possible obstacles, including competition, conflicts of interest, and regulatory compliance. Partnerships between fintech and established financial institutions will continue to be essential to innovation and expansion in the digital economy as fintech reshapes the economic landscape.

Successful partnership case studies

Adequate partnership case studies provide insightful information on how traditional financial institutions, fintech companies, and other stakeholders may work together to drive innovation, increase access to financial services, and promote sustainable growth. These case studies demonstrate how strategic alliances can use complementary skills, assets, and knowledge to solve problems and benefit stakeholders and customers.

The collaboration between PayPal and Visa, two major payment sector participants, is one noteworthy case study. A strategic agreement between PayPal and Visa was established in 2016 to improve global digital payment experiences for customers and merchants. As a condition of the collaboration, PayPal consented to become a member of Visa's digital wallet initiative, allowing customers to easily connect their PayPal accounts to Visa-branded credit and debit cards. Additionally, to promote the use of digital payments and improve security and convenience for customers and merchants, PayPal and Visa decided to work together on projects including tokenization, data sharing, and co-marketing. The collaboration between fintech and traditional financial institutions can open up new avenues and spur innovation in the payments business, as evidenced by the partnership between PayPal and Visa.

The collaboration between Apple and Goldman Sachs to introduce the Apple Card, a new credit card ideal for the digital era, is another interesting case study. In 2019, Goldman Sachs and Apple collaborated to develop a co-branded credit card with cutting-edge features, including no fees, daily cashback benefits, and budgeting tools that work smoothly with Apple Pay. The Apple Card is a unique and distinctive product that appeals to tech-savvy consumers. It combines Apple's technological prowess and Goldman Sachs' banking knowledge. Goldman Sachs and Apple produced a successful product that upended the conventional credit card market and drew in millions of users globally by combining their unique strengths and talents.

Furthermore, the alliance between Ant Group and Vanguard is a strong illustration of how technology and established financial institutions can work together to democratize investing access. In 2020, Ant Group, the financial technology division of Alibaba Group, collaborated with Vanguard, a global investment management firm, to introduce a novel digital investing platform targeted at Chinese retail investors. The Ant Fortune platform utilizes the technological infrastructure of Ant Group and the investment experience of Vanguard to provide low-cost investment products, including index funds and ETFs, to Chinese consumers. Ant Group and Vanguard's partnership exemplifies how fintech and traditional financial institutions may work together to utilize technology and knowledge better to increase investment accessibility and enable people to reach their financial objectives.

In addition, JPMorgan Chase and OnDeck Capital's cooperation illustrates how a traditional bank and a fintech lending platform work together to serve small company clients better. To introduce "Chase Business Quick Capital," a new online lending platform that offers small business clients quick and easy access to short-term loans, JPMorgan Chase and OnDeck Capital teamed together in 2015. The platform uses the technology and underwriting skills of OnDeck Capital to expedite the loan application and approval process, giving small businesses access to capital in an effective and timely manner. JPMorgan Chase was able to access underserved small company consumers and broaden its product offerings by collaborating with OnDeck Capital. This illustrates the potential for fintech and traditional financial institutions to work together to address small businesses' financing requirements.

Finally, successful partnership case studies demonstrate how cooperation amongst fintech companies, established financial institutions and other stakeholders may revolutionize innovation, increase access to financial services, and promote long-term growth. These case studies show how strategic partnerships can use complementary strengths, resources, and expertise to create value for customers and stakeholders. Examples of such partnerships include those between fintech startups and traditional banks, investment firms like Goldman Sachs and Apple, and payment giants like PayPal and Visa. Partnerships will continue to be a vital component of innovation and development in the digital economy as fintech transforms the financial landscape.

CHAPTER XII

The Future of Fintech

Emerging trends and technologies

Emerging trends and technologies that have the potential to transform the financial services sector ultimately will continue to impact the fintech landscape in the future. The development of artificial intelligence (AI) and machine learning (ML) technology is one of the significant themes influencing the direction of fintech. Financial services could see substantial changes from fraud detection and investment research to risk management and client service due to AI and ML. Financial institutions may automate repetitive activities, obtain better insights into consumer behavior, and customize solutions to each customer's specific needs by utilizing AI-powered algorithms. Furthermore, by offering individualized support and recommendations in real-time across numerous channels, AI-driven chatbots and virtual assistants are increasingly used to improve the customer experience.

An additional noteworthy development influencing fintech's future is the expanding use of blockchain technology. Blockchain, the underlying technology of cryptocurrencies like Bitcoin, provides a decentralized and transparent record system that allows for safe and unchangeable transactions. Financial institutions are investigating how blockchain might reduce costs, minimize risks, and increase efficiency by streamlining procedures, including trade financing, securities settlement, and cross-border payments. Furthermore, using blockchain-based smart contracts to automate and enforce contracts allows faster more transparent transactions without intermediaries.

Furthermore, the financial services sector is experiencing a cashless revolution due to the widespread use of mobile wallets and digital payments. Consumers are using digital payment systems more frequently to conduct transactions swiftly, securely, and conveniently due to the proliferation of smartphones and internet connectivity. Consumers worldwide are starting to favor mobile wallets —such as Apple Pay, Google Pay, and Samsung Pay—for their ability to make contactless payments, peer-to-peer transfers, and loyalty benefits. Furthermore, the fintech ecosystem is seeing a surge in innovation and cooperation due to the adoption of open banking and application programming interfaces (APIs), which facilitate seamless connections between financial services and outside apps.

Additionally, democratizing wealth management and investing through robo-advisors and digital wealth platforms characterizes the fintech of the future. With the help of automated and customized investing advice, robo-advisors—driven by AI and ML algorithms—help individual investors attain their financial objectives and diversify their holdings. Furthermore, various financial products, including equities, bonds, exchange-traded funds (ETFs), and mutual funds, are accessible through digital wealth platforms, enabling investors to manage their wealth and customize their portfolios online. In addition, social media platforms for investing are becoming increasingly well-liked. These platforms allow investors to exchange ideas, work together on investment plans, and benefit from one another's experiences.

Furthermore, as financial institutions attempt to traverse ever-more complex regulatory frameworks and guarantee compliance with changing legislation, regulatory and compliance technologies, or RegTech, are emerging as a critical area of innovation in the fintech space. RegTech solutions use artificial intelligence (AI), machine learning (ML), and big data analytics to automate regulatory reporting, monitor transactions for questionable activity, and better manage compliance risks. By utilizing RegTech solutions, financial institutions can lower costs, increase accountability and transparency, and streamline compliance procedures.

To sum up, new developments in technology and trends that have the potential to transform the financial services sector and improve client satisfaction will define the fintech landscape in the future. Fintech is accelerating innovation and change in several industries, from digital payments and robo-advisors to blockchain technology and artificial intelligence. It is also creating new chances for efficiency, growth, and cooperation. Financial institutions and technology providers need to be competitive and satisfy customers' changing needs in the digital age by embracing innovation, using emerging technologies, and adapting to these changes as fintech continues to expand.

Predictions for the next decade

Many predictions for the next ten years in technology and finance are driven by continued technological improvements, shifting consumer preferences, and regulatory developments. The ongoing emergence of digital currencies and central bank digital currencies (CBDCs) is one of the main predictions. As cryptocurrencies like Bitcoin and Ethereum gain more traction, central banks worldwide are considering launching virtual money. Potential advantages of CBDCs include lower transaction costs, more financial inclusion, and more monetary policy transparency. Adopting CBDCs may also change the nature of international payments by offering a substitute for fiat currencies and facilitating cross-border transactions that are quicker, less expensive, and more effective.

An additional forecast for the upcoming ten years is the extensive implementation of open banking and data-sharing programs. Open banking fosters innovation and competition in the financial services sector by granting third-party developers access to bank data via APIs. Open banking is making it easier for fintech companies to develop new products and services that improve customer experience and advance financial inclusion by giving them access to consumer data from various banks and financial institutions. Furthermore, by offering consumers the power to manage and share their financial data with third-party providers, data-sharing initiatives like Australia's Consumer Data Right (CDR) and Europe's Payment Services Directive 2 (PSD2) foster greater competition, transparency, and innovation in the financial ecosystem.

Furthermore, fintech is expected to grow throughout the next ten years, entering underserved demographics and emerging regions. Fintech firms increasingly focus on underbanked and unbanked populations in emerging economies because of the widespread use of smartphones and internet connectivity. These companies provide digital financial services like insurance, microloans, and mobile payments. Furthermore, promoting digital financial inclusion and empowering individuals and small companies in developing nations to access and utilize formal financial services are spearheaded by programs like the Gates Foundation's Level One Project and the United Nations' Better Than Cash Alliance.

Furthermore, forecasts for the ensuing ten years indicate that machine learning (ML) and artificial intelligence (AI) will be widely used in various financial services industries. Financial institutions will be able to make faster, more informed decisions and provide more individualized experiences for their clients due to the potential for AI and ML to revolutionize operations like investment research, risk management, fraud detection, and customer support. Furthermore, developments in conversational AI and natural language processing (NLP) are opening the door for creating chatbots and virtual assistants who can instantly converse with clients and offer them individualized support and recommendations.

Furthermore, more regulatory monitoring and examination of fintech companies is probably in store for the next ten years, especially in areas like consumer protection, cybersecurity, and data privacy. Regulators want to ensure innovation is balanced with responsibility and transparency as fintech continues to upend traditional financial services. Regulations like the EU's Revised Payment Services Directive (PSD2) and Australia's Open Banking regime are encouraging competition and innovation in the economic ecosystem, while initiatives like Europe's General Data Protection Regulation (GDPR) and California's Consumer Privacy Act (CCPA) are placing stricter requirements on how businesses collect, use, and protect consumer data.

In conclusion, forecasts for the financial and technological fields for the ensuing ten years suggest that innovation, disruption, and change will persist. The financial services sector will face many opportunities and difficulties during the next ten years, including the broad acceptance of digital currencies, open banking, fintech's growth into emerging economies, and the growing usage of AI and ML technologies. Stakeholders must embrace innovation, adjust to how technology changes the financial landscape, and work together to build a more transparent, efficient, and inclusive financial ecosystem that benefits everyone.

Potential impact on the global financial system

It is impossible to overestimate the possible influence of different financial and technological trends and advancements on the world economic system. The financial landscape is changing dramatically as the globe becomes more digitally linked and integrated. These changes will have a significant impact on individuals, businesses, and economies worldwide.

The emergence of digital currencies and blockchain technology is one significant factor that could impact the global financial system. In recent years, cryptocurrencies like Bitcoin and Ethereum have gained a lot of interest and challenged conventional ideas about money and finance. The underlying technology of cryptocurrencies, blockchain, provides a transparent and decentralized ledger system that can completely transform trade finance, securities settlement, payments, and other facets of the financial system. Central banks worldwide are investigating the prospect of creating their digital currencies, or central bank digital currencies, or CBDCs, which can completely change how money is made, distributed, and controlled. Furthermore, blockchain technology can lower costs, boost efficiency, and lessen risk in financial transactions, resulting in increased security, transparency, and confidence in the world economic system.

The rise in fintech and digital-first banking could have an additional effect on the global financial system. Fintech businesses are upending traditional financial services and fostering competition and creativity by utilizing technology to create creative financial goods and services. Fintech solutions are changing how customers access and use financial services, from peer-to-peer lending platforms and robo-advisors to digital wallets and mobile payments, resulting in increased financial inclusion and empowerment. Furthermore, implementing open banking and data-sharing programs facilitates increased cooperation and integration among fintech companies, conventional financial institutions, and other relevant parties, generating novel prospects for innovation and collaboration within the worldwide financial ecosystem.

Moreover, the growing regulatory monitoring and oversight of fintech companies and digital currencies could impact the global financial system. Regulators face further difficulties as fintech continues to upend conventional financial services in data privacy, cybersecurity, and consumer protection. Stricter guidelines are being placed on how businesses gather, utilize, and safeguard customer data by initiatives like the US's California Consumer Privacy Act (CCPA) and the General Data Protection Regulation (GDPR) in Europe. Similar to this, laws like Australia's Open Banking policy and Europe's Revised Payment Services Directive (PSD2) encourage competition and innovation in the financial sector while protecting the economic system's security and integrity. In addition, authorities are keeping a careful eye on the development of blockchain technology and digital currencies to ensure there are no systemic hazards to the integrity and stability of the world financial system.

In conclusion, trends and advancements in finance and technology have the potential to impact the global financial system significantly. The emergence of digital currencies and blockchain technology, the spread of fintech solutions, and heightened regulatory oversight are fundamentally altering the worldwide landscape of financial services accessibility, provision, and regulation. These changes present new dangers and opportunities for innovation and growth. Still, they also bring fascinating new difficulties that must be addressed through responsible innovation, cooperative efforts, and effective regulation. It is critical to acknowledge the possible effects on the global financial system as we look to the future of technology and finance and to collaborate to keep it resilient, stable, and open to all.

CHAPTER XIII

Leading Fintech Companies

Profiles of major Fintech companies

Prominent fintech enterprises have surfaced as crucial entities in the swiftly changing domain of finance and technology, propelling ingenuity, upheaval, and metamorphosis throughout diverse segments of the financial services sector. These businesses combine technology, data analytics, and user-centered design to create cutting-edge goods and services that adapt to the changing demands of industries and customers in the modern digital economy. Several prominent fintech firms, including PayPal, Square, Stripe, Ant Group, and Robinhood, are making noteworthy advancements in the sector.

One of the forerunners in digital wallets and online payment processing is PayPal, which was established in 1998. It is a well-known online payment brand thanks to its user-friendly infrastructure and widespread adoption across e-commerce websites and mobile apps. Peer-to-peer payments, bill payments, merchant services, and secure payment sending and receiving are just a few of the financial services the company offers to consumers and organizations. Additionally, PayPal has broadened its portfolio with well-timed acquisitions, such as the well-known mobile payment network Venmo, which has allowed it to enter the expanding digital payment and mobile wallet markets.

Established in 2009 by Jack Dorsey, a co-founder of Twitter, Square is a prominent fintech enterprise that has revolutionized how businesses receive payments and handle their accounts. The Square Reader, the company's primary product, is a compact, handheld gadget that enables establishments to pay for credit cards via a tablet or smartphone. Square provides a range of financial services, such as company loans, payroll processing, point-of-sale software, and payment processing. Additionally, Square's peer-to-peer payment software, Square Cash, has become popular among users because of its ease of use and convenience, which has increased the company's visibility and influence within the fintech sector.

Irish brothers Patrick and John Collison launched Stripe in 2010. Since then, it has become a significant force in online payment processing, enabling transactions for millions of companies worldwide. Businesses can accept payments online, through mobile apps, and in person using Stripe's simple-to-integrate payment infrastructure, all while giving customers a safe and straightforward checkout process. Stripe is a one-stop shop for companies wishing to grow and penetrate new markets because it provides various extra services like international payments, fraud detection, and subscription billing.

Alibaba Group established Ant Group, formerly known as Ant Financial, a Chinese fintech company, in 2014. One of the world's most extensive mobile payment networks, Alipay, is run by Ant Group. It has over a billion users and offers various financial services, such as loans, wealth management, insurance, and digital wallets. Alipay has become a dominant force in China's digital payments sector thanks to its user-friendly interface, smooth integration with Alibaba's e-commerce platforms, and cutting-edge technologies like facial recognition payments. Furthermore, Ant Group has strengthened its standing as a top fintech business internationally by branching into other financial services, including asset management and digital banking.

Established in 2013 by Baiju Bhatt and Vladimir Tenev, Robinhood has caused a stir in the traditional brokerage sector with its commission-free trading platform and easy-to-use mobile app. A new generation of investors may purchase and sell stocks, options, cryptocurrencies, and exchange-traded funds (ETFs) on Robinhood's platform without paying commissions. Furthermore, millions of customers have been drawn to Robinhood by its cutting-edge features, which include customizable notifications, automated dividend reinvestment, and fractional share trading. As a result, the company is now among the fastest-growing fintech startups in the US.

In conclusion, the financial services sector is undergoing innovation, disruption, and transformation thanks to the efforts of top fintech firms like PayPal, Square, Stripe, Ant Group, and Robinhood. These businesses combine technology, data analytics, and user-centered design to create cutting-edge goods and services that adapt to the changing demands of businesses and customers in the modern digital economy. These businesses are well-positioned to take advantage of new opportunities as fintech continues transforming the financial industry and maintaining its growth and global impact trajectory.

Their innovations and market impact

Leading fintech startups have significantly changed the financial services industry and transformed how individuals and organizations deal with money through their innovations and market effects. These businesses have democratized access to financial services, expedited digital transformation, and increased industry competition and efficiency by introducing disruptive technology, user-centric solutions, and creative business models.

The advent of digital payment platforms and mobile wallets is one major innovation that has significantly impacted the market. Fintech firms, including PayPal, Square, and Ant Group, have created user-friendly mobile applications that facilitate money transfers, online and in-store purchases, and smooth financial management from smartphones. In addition to making transactions more manageable and more accessible, these digital payment systems have promoted financial inclusion by giving underprivileged groups access to banking services that they might not have otherwise had.

In addition, fintech companies invented peer-to-peer (P2P) lending and crowdfunding, which enable individuals and enterprises to lend and borrow money directly through online platforms. Businesses such as Lending Club, Prosper, and Funding Circle have established online marketplaces that pair borrowers and investors. By eliminating the middleman, these platforms lower the expense and complexity of conventional lending procedures. Due to this invention, financing that would not have been available through traditional banks is now accessible to people and small enterprises.

Fintech firms have also brought cutting-edge wealth management and investing solutions that democratize access to financial markets and customized investment guidance. Algorithms and automation are used by robo-advisors, such as Betterment, Wealthfront, and Acorns, to create affordable, diversified investment portfolios that are customized to the risk tolerance and goals of individual investors. A larger audience may now invest more easily thanks to these platforms, especially millennials and novice investors who may have put off the complexity and high cost of traditional wealth management services.

In addition, the financial sector has seen a paradigm shift due to the rise of blockchain technology and cryptocurrencies, with firms like Coinbase, Binance, and Gemini setting the standard for safe and convenient online marketplaces for purchasing, trading, and storing digital assets. Blockchain technology makes record-keeping transparent and impenetrable, facilitating secure, effective transactions without intermediaries. With their ability to challenge established fiat currencies and financial systems, cryptocurrencies such as Bitcoin and Ethereum have become widely accepted as substitutes for traditional stores of value and means of trade.

Fintech businesses have also developed creative solutions for risk management, fraud detection, and regulatory compliance by utilizing data analytics and machine learning. Businesses such as Ayasdi, Feedzai, and Chainalysis employ sophisticated algorithms to instantly evaluate enormous volumes of data and spot trends and irregularities that could point to fraud or legal infractions. Financial institutions have benefited from these developments by reducing losses, mitigating risks, and adhering to stricter regulations.

In summary, the financial services industry has undergone a significant transformation due to prominent fintech companies' innovations and market influence. This has increased accessibility, efficiency, and transparency in how individuals and organizations manage their finances. Fintech companies have introduced disruptive technologies and business models that have democratized access to financial services, accelerated digital transformation, and revolutionized how people interact with money in the modern digital age. Examples include digital payment platforms, peer-to-peer lending, robo-advisors, and blockchain technology. These businesses are well-positioned to continue influencing the direction of finance as fintech develops and to spur more innovation and rivalry within the sector.

Lessons learned from their success

Important lessons that may be learned and applied to other industries and business contexts can be learned from the success of top fintech startups. These lessons emphasize how crucial innovation, customer-centricity, agility, and strategic alliances are to foster development and sustainability in today's quickly changing corporate environment.

Being innovative and disruptive is essential to staying ahead of the curve, as seen by the success of fintech companies. To adapt their goods and services to the changing demands of consumers and businesses, these organizations have shown a willingness to test the boundaries of new technology, question established conventions, and refine their offerings. Fintech companies have managed to stay ahead of the competition and stand out in a crowded industry by adopting an innovative culture and cultivating a mindset of constant learning and adaptability.

Furthermore, the accomplishments of fintech companies highlight how crucial it is to put the consumer's needs first and provide value-added solutions that truly alleviate problems and benefit customers in noticeable ways. Thanks to the user-friendly platforms and seamless experiences created by fintech companies like PayPal, Square, and Robinhood, financial services are now more accessible for consumers and businesses to access and utilize. These businesses have developed a robust and devoted clientele and sustained growth over time by putting the needs of their users front and center during the product development process and using user feedback to inform future developments.

Fintech companies' success also emphasizes how crucial it is to be flexible and agile to adjust to shifting consumer preferences and market conditions. Companies need to be able to quickly innovate, pivot, and iterate in today's fast-paced business climate to keep up with developing trends, threats from competitors, and changes in regulations. Whether branching out into new product lines, breaking into new geographic markets, or forming strategic alliances with other industry players, fintech companies have proven exceptionally adept at pivoting and adapting their business models in response to shifting market conditions.

Furthermore, the success of fintech businesses emphasizes how crucial strategic alliances and teamwork are to accelerating growth and scalability. To increase their reach, open up new markets, and use complementary skills and abilities, fintech companies have partnered with banks, IT firms, and other industry participants. By working together with established incumbents, fintech startups have earned credibility and confidence, reached out to preexisting client bases, and accelerated their growth trajectory.

Furthermore, the prosperity of fintech enterprises underscores the significance of adhering to regulations and managing risks to establish confidence and trustworthiness with stakeholders and customers. Since the fintech sector is heavily regulated, adhering to the law is essential to the growth and viability of these businesses. Prioritizing regulatory compliance and making significant investments in risk management frameworks puts firms in a better position to manage regulatory obstacles, reduce legal and reputational risks, and forge enduring bonds with partners and clients.

To sum up, the prosperity of top fintech firms provides insightful insights transferable to many company settings and sectors. These lessons emphasize how crucial it is to drive development and sustainability in today's quickly changing company environment through innovation, customer-centricity, agility, strategic partnerships, regulatory compliance, and risk management. Businesses may set themselves up for success and prosper in a market that is becoming more competitive and dynamic by accepting these principles and embracing a philosophy of constant learning and adaptation.

CHAPTER XIV

Fintech in Emerging Markets

The role of Fintech in emerging economies

Financial technology, or fintech, is becoming increasingly important in emerging nations. It promotes economic growth, development, and financial inclusion in areas where traditional banking infrastructure may be scarce or unreachable. Fintech solutions offer various financial services, such as digital payments, mobile banking, peer-to-peer lending, and microfinance, to individuals and businesses in emerging countries using technology, data analytics, and creative business models.

Fintech plays a significant role in emerging nations by tackling the issue of financial exclusion by facilitating access to formal financial services for marginalized groups. Many people in emerging economies do not have access to traditional banking services like credit cards, savings accounts, and loans because of exorbitant fees, inadequate physical infrastructure, and strict qualifying standards. Fintech businesses are reaching unbanked and underbanked populations using digital platforms and mobile technologies to make it easier and more affordable for them to manage their finances, make payments, open accounts, and obtain loans.

Fintech is also fostering innovation in the provision of financial services in developing nations, opening up new avenues for people and companies to get and use economic goods and services customized to meet their unique requirements. People in emerging nations may now send and receive money, pay bills, and access other financial services via their mobile phones thanks to mobile money networks like M-Pesa in Kenya and bKash in

Bangladesh. Peer-to-peer lending platforms such as Kiva and Zidisha facilitate the connection between global investors and borrowers in emerging economies, thereby furnishing much-needed funding for the expansion and prosperity of small enterprises and entrepreneurs.

Fintech is also vital to advancing financial inclusion and resilience among underprivileged groups in emerging countries, such as women, young people, and rural areas. Fintech businesses enable people and communities to manage financial risks better, save money, and obtain credit by giving them access to digital financial services. This improves people's quality of life and future possibilities. To help people in emerging markets who might not have access to traditional banking services, digital microfinance platforms such as Tala and Branch are offering small loans. These loans allow the borrowers to invest in things like healthcare, education, and income-generating ventures.

Furthermore, by encouraging entrepreneurship, innovation, and investment in novel and underrepresented economic sectors, fintech accelerates economic growth and development in emerging nations. Fintech firms are utilizing technology and data analytics in emerging economies to create inventive solutions for local problems, like small and medium-sized enterprises (SMEs) needing more access to cash, insurance, and credit. Fintech is also drawing capital and investment into developing nations, promoting economic expansion and opening up new avenues for wealth creation and employment creation.

In summary, fintech is transforming emerging economies by promoting financial inclusion, economic expansion, and development in areas where access to traditional banking infrastructure may be restricted. Fintech enables people and communities to create more resilient and prosperous futures by stimulating investment, supporting innovation, and granting access to digital financial services. As it develops further and becomes more prevalent in developing nations, fintech has the potential to open up new doors and bring about positive change for millions of people worldwide.

Case studies from Asia, Africa, and Latin America

Case studies from Latin America, Africa, and Asia shed important light on how fintech revolutionizes financial inclusion, economic growth, and poverty reduction in emerging nations. The case above studies showcases the inventive strategies, obstacles, and accomplishments of fintech enterprises and endeavors in catering to the distinct requirements and limitations of heterogeneous communities in these areas.

Mobile money apps, such as bKash in Bangladesh and M-Pesa in Kenya, have entirely changed how individuals interact and handle their finances across Asia, especially in underdeveloped and rural areas. Users of mobile phones can send and receive money, pay bills, and access other financial services with M-Pesa, a service introduced by Safaricom in Kenya in 2007. Millions of Kenyans, especially smallholder farmers and rural business owners, have benefited from the platform by obtaining official financial services for the first time, which has improved their ability to save, invest, and expand their enterprises. Similarly, millions of unbanked and underbanked people and businesses nationwide are served by bKash, introduced by BRAC Bank in Bangladesh in 2011, and has grown to become the nation's top mobile money provider. These case studies show how mobile money can significantly advance financial inclusion and economic empowerment in developing countries.

Peer-to-peer lending websites like Kiva and Zidisha unite global investors and African borrowers, funding small businesses and entrepreneurs to expand and prosper. Since its founding in 2005, Kiva has helped people worldwide access inexpensive finance for various needs, such as healthcare, education, and agriculture, by allowing consumers to lend as little as $25 to borrowers in more than 80 countries. Similarly, Zidisha, established in 2009, connects lenders and borrowers directly in poor nations via a peer-to-peer lending model, doing away with conventional intermediaries and lowering the cost and complexity of borrowing. Peer-to-peer lending has the potential to unleash money and generate chances for economic growth and development in Africa and other regions, as demonstrated by these case studies.

Fintech companies are upending traditional banking and financial services in Latin America by giving customers creative, user-friendly alternatives to conventional banks, such as Mercado Pago in Argentina and Nubank in Brazil. Established in 2013, Nubank provides various online and mobile banking services, such as personal loans, savings accounts, and credit cards. Millions of Brazilians have flocked to the organization because it provides precise costs, cheaper interest rates, and better customer service than traditional banks. Similarly, Mercado Pago— introduced by Mercado Libre in 2003—has grown to become one of Latin America's top digital payment systems, allowing users to send and receive money, pay their bills, and make in-person and online purchases. These case studies show how fintech is revolutionizing financial services and consumer behavior in Latin America, benefiting millions and increasing accessibility, cost, and convenience.

Finally, case studies from Latin America, Africa, and Asia offer convincing proof of the revolutionary influence of fintech on financial inclusion, economic growth, and poverty reduction in emerging nations. Fintech businesses and initiatives are transforming how people access and use financial services, opening up new opportunities and bringing about positive change for people and communities worldwide. Examples of these include peer-to-peer lending, digital banking, payment solutions, and mobile money platforms. Fintech can have a long-lasting effect and promote equitable progress and prosperity for millions of people in emerging nations as it develops and broadens its reach.

Challenges and opportunities in these markets

Emerging markets present numerous opportunities and challenges for the acceptance and growth of fintech. Asia, Africa, and Latin America present distinct chances for fintech enterprises to tackle urgent financial requirements and promote equitable development. However, to fully fulfill fintech's potential in these regions, a number of critical difficulties must be overcome.

In emerging nations, people need more financial literacy and traditional banking infrastructure. Essential financial services, including loans, insurance, and savings accounts, are inaccessible to many people in these areas. Furthermore, especially in underprivileged and marginalized groups, there is sometimes a need for more knowledge and comprehension regarding fintech solutions. To overcome these obstacles, fintech companies must fund education and awareness campaigns to raise people's understanding of digital financial services' advantages and dangers and foster a sense of trust in these platforms.

Regulatory limitations and compliance standards can also provide severe difficulties for fintech businesses that operate in developing nations. The intricate, dispersed, and dynamic regulatory environments in these areas can pose challenges and obstacles to entrance for fintech enterprises. Additionally, the expenses associated with regulatory compliance may need to be lowered for smaller fintech businesses, which would hinder their capacity to grow and develop. Regulatory obstacles, however, also offer cooperation and partnership opportunities between regulators and fintech firms to create lucid, encouraging frameworks that enable innovation while preserving financial stability and consumer protection.

Fintech solution uptake and usage in emerging nations can also be impeded by infrastructure and connection problems. Access to digital financial services may be restricted for many people living in underserved and rural areas due to a lack of dependable mobile devices and internet connectivity. Furthermore, infrastructure problems may also affect fintech platforms' dependability and security, raising issues with cybersecurity and data privacy. To ensure that all people and communities can access and benefit from fintech solutions, addressing these issues needs investments in digital infrastructure, such as increasing internet access and enhancing network security and dependability.

Nevertheless, fintech companies may leverage emerging markets to propel financial inclusion, economic growth, and innovation, even in the face of these challenges. For fintech goods and services, the sizable underprivileged populations in these areas offer a sizable untapped market. Given the increasing uptake of digital platforms and mobile technology in emerging economies, fintech companies can also take advantage of these channels to expand their customer base and offer creative solutions.
Fintech companies might find fertile ground to develop and test new business models and technology in emerging markets because these regions frequently exhibit high innovation and entrepreneurial activity levels.

Moreover, emerging regions have dynamic and diversified economies, which gives fintech companies a chance to provide customized solutions to fulfill the specific needs of various populations and solve local problems. African fintech startups, for instance, have created creative solutions for financing agriculture, microfinance, and healthcare by utilizing alternative data sources and mobile technologies to target underprivileged sectors and communities. Fintech enterprises operating in Latin America have created digital banking and payment systems to cater to the needs of underbanked and unbanked individuals, promoting financial inclusion and self-determination.

In conclusion, fintech businesses looking to promote financial inclusion, economic growth, and innovation will find both possibilities and obstacles in emerging nations. Although infrastructure problems, regulatory restrictions, and inadequate financial literacy are formidable obstacles, they also offer cooperation, creativity, and partnership opportunities. Fintech companies may drive positive change for individuals and communities across Asia, Africa, and Latin America by tackling these concerns and using the particular opportunities in these markets. This can open up new sources of development and influence.

CHAPTER XV

Fintech for Small and Medium Enterprises

Fintech solutions for SMEs

Small and medium-sized enterprises' (SMEs') particular financial demands and issues can now be effectively addressed with the help of fintech solutions. In economies worldwide, SMEs are essential for fostering innovation, job creation, and economic growth. Nevertheless, they frequently encounter challenges when obtaining finance, managing cash flow, and using standard banking services. Fintech solutions enable SMEs to grow, prosper, and compete in today's digital economy by providing them with creative, easily accessible, and reasonably priced alternatives to traditional banking and financial services.

Financing access is one of the main areas where fintech solutions are having a significant influence on SMEs. Many small and medium-sized enterprises have trouble getting loans from traditional banks because of the strict qualifying standards, limitations on collateral, and drawn-out approval procedures. Fintech businesses are creating creative loan solutions tailored to SMEs' unique requirements by utilizing technology and alternative data sources. For instance, peer-to-peer lending sites such as Funding Circle and LendingClub allow SMEs to connect directly with investors who are prepared to give funds, avoiding traditional banks and lowering the cost and complexity of borrowing. Fintech companies also use machine learning algorithms and data analytics to analyze credit risk more precisely and quickly. This allows them to lend money to SMEs that traditional banks might have passed over or underserved.

Fintech technologies also transform how SMEs handle their funds, optimize processes, and boost productivity. SMEs can access digital banking services through mobile apps and web portals from digital banking platforms such as Revolut, Tide, and Azlo. These services include online account opening, payments, invoicing, and cost management. These solutions give SMEs instant access to their financial data, empowering them to handle cash flow more skillfully and make quicker, more informed decisions. Fintech solutions also automate repetitive financial operations like tax compliance, bookkeeping, and accounting, giving SMEs more time and resources to concentrate on their core competencies and business expansion.

Fintech solutions are also helping disenfranchised and underserved SMEs, especially in emerging economies, become more financially inclusive and empowered. SMEs encounter numerous obstacles in developing nations when attempting to obtain formal financial services, such as inadequate physical infrastructure, exorbitant expenses, and regulatory limitations. Fintech companies are reaching small and medium-sized enterprises (SMEs) in underserved and distant locations using digital platforms and mobile technologies. This allows SMEs to access banking services, make payments, and apply for financing without visiting a physical bank branch. Furthermore, through trade finance, currency hedging, and cross-border payments, fintech solutions open up worldwide markets and allow SMEs to be part of global value chains.

Fintech solutions also encourage innovation and entrepreneurship among SMEs by giving them access to many resources and tools that facilitate the development and expansion of their businesses. SMEs can raise money from a global community of backers using crowdfunding sites like Kickstarter and Indiegogo to fund product development, marketing campaigns, and growth plans. Fintech solutions also give SMEs access to digital marketing tools, market data, and advanced analytics to aid in opportunity identification, customer understanding, and competitive strategy development. Fintech solutions also encourage increased cooperation and collaborations among SMEs, giving them access to new markets, resource sharing, and more efficient company scaling.

To sum up, fintech solutions revolutionize how SMEs obtain financing, handle money, and expand enterprises. Fintech enterprises enable small and medium-sized enterprises (SMEs) to surmount growth obstacles and contend in the contemporary digital economy by offering inventive, easily accessible, and economically viable substitutes for conventional banking and financial services. Furthermore, fintech solutions promote greater financial inclusion and empowerment among underrepresented and underserved SMEs, especially in emerging markets. Fintech can open up new growth and opportunity channels for SMEs worldwide as it develops and spreads, promoting innovation, economic growth, and job creation.

Impact on SME growth and development

Fintech has significantly impacted the growth and development of small and medium-sized enterprises (SMEs), changing how these companies acquire financing, handle their finances, and do business in the current digital economy. Fintech solutions have enabled SMEs to surpass conventional growth constraints and compete more successfully in international markets, promoting innovation, economic development, and job creation.

Access to financing is one of the most significant effects of fintech on the expansion and development of SMEs. SMEs have historically had difficulty obtaining funding from traditional banks at reasonable rates because of the banks' strict qualifying standards, limitations on collateral, and drawn-out approval procedures. By utilizing technology and alternative data sources to provide creative loan solutions catered to the requirements of SMEs, fintech companies have upended this market. Compared to traditional banks, peer-to-peer lending platforms, crowdfunding sites, and digital banks provide SMEs with faster, more transparent, and more affordable access to cash, allowing them to invest in expansion growth and take advantage of new opportunities.

Furthermore, fintech solutions promote greater financial inclusion and empowerment among underrepresented and underserved SMEs, especially in emerging markets. SMEs encounter numerous obstacles in developing nations when attempting to obtain formal financial services, such as inadequate physical infrastructure, exorbitant expenses, and regulatory limitations. Fintech companies are reaching small and medium-sized enterprises (SMEs) in underserved and distant locations using digital platforms and mobile technologies. This allows SMEs to access banking services, make payments, and apply for financing without visiting a physical bank branch. Due to SMEs' increased ability to obtain funding, these areas see increased economic growth and development due to their investments in new technology, market expansion, and job creation.

Fintech solutions are also revolutionizing SMEs' financial management, streamlining business operations, and increasing productivity. Through mobile apps and web portals, digital banking platforms provide SMEs various services, including online account opening, payments, invoicing, and cost management. These solutions give

SMEs instant access to their financial data, empowering them to handle cash flow more skillfully and make quicker, more informed decisions. Fintech solutions also automate repetitive financial duties like tax compliance, bookkeeping, and accounting, giving SMEs more time and resources to concentrate on their core business operations and expansion.

Fintech solutions also encourage entrepreneurship and innovation among SMEs by giving them access to many resources and tools that facilitate the development and expansion of their businesses. Through crowdfunding platforms, small and medium-sized enterprises (SMEs) can raise money from a worldwide network of backers to support marketing campaigns, product development, and expansion plans. Fintech solutions also give SMEs access to digital marketing tools, market data, and advanced analytics to aid in opportunity identification, customer understanding, and competitive strategy development. Fintech promotes economic diversification, long-term sustainable development, and job creation by giving SMEs the resources they require to innovate and expand.

To sum up, fintech has revolutionized the growth and development of SMEs by enabling them to surmount conventional growth obstacles and more successfully participate in the current digital economy. Fintech is accelerating economic growth, job creation, and innovation in economies worldwide by facilitating access to capital, promoting financial inclusion, streamlining processes, and encouraging entrepreneurship and creativity. Fintech can open up new growth and opportunity channels for SMEs as it develops and spreads, promoting equitable and sustainable development for years.

Successful SME-focused Fintech platforms

Effective fintech platforms catering to small and medium-sized businesses (SMEs) have become indispensable instruments for tackling the distinct financial requirements and obstacles these businesses encounter globally. These platforms use data analytics, technology, and creative business strategies to help SMEs get funding, improve operations, and spur expansion. A number of noteworthy instances of their effective implementation have illustrated the revolutionary effect that SME-focused fintech platforms may have on SMEs and the overall economy.

One such website is Funding Circle, a peer-to-peer lending network that links small and medium-sized enterprises (SMEs) needing funding with direct lenders. Since its founding in 2010, Funding Circle has helped SMEs in the US, UK, and other markets obtain billions of dollars in loans, allowing them to grow, expand, and generate employment. The platform provides loans to SMEs who would have been disregarded or mistreated by traditional banks by utilizing technology and data analytics to analyze credit risk more precisely and effectively. Funding Circle has aided hundreds of SMEs in realizing their growth potential and boosting local economies by giving them access to financing at reasonable rates.

Xero is a cloud-based accounting software platform that assists SMEs in managing their money, streamlining operations, and increasing productivity. It is another effective fintech platform targeted towards SMEs. Xero, founded in 2006, has grown to be the world's largest accounting software supplier for small and medium-sized businesses, with millions of users in more than 180 nations. The platform provides several functionalities that may be accessed via an intuitive mobile app and user-friendly interface, such as payroll, spending management, invoicing, and financial reporting. Xero helps SMEs save time and money by automating repetitive financial chores and giving them real-time visibility into their accounts. This allows them to concentrate on their core company operations and expansion.

Furthermore, Square, a 2009 startup, has become a prominent fintech platform for small and medium-sized enterprises (SMEs), offering a variety of point-of-sale, company management, and payment processing services. Through a single platform, SMEs can track sales, manage inventory, take card payments, and access finance thanks to Square's portfolio of goods and services. The creative hardware and software solutions offered by the company are made to cater to small and medium-sized enterprises (SMEs) across a range of sectors, including e-commerce, professional services, retail, and hospitality. Square has enabled millions of small company owners and entrepreneurs to thrive in the current competitive market by providing low-cost, user-friendly solutions.

Furthermore, another well-known SME-focused fintech platform that offers accounting, payroll, and financial management solutions for SMEs is QuickBooks, which Intuit owns. SMEs can easily manage their finances, track spending, and generate financial reports with the help of QuickBooks' cloud-based software, which helps them stay organized and make wise decisions. In addition, the platform provides SMEs with capabilities like inventory management, tax preparation, and invoicing. With millions of customers globally, QuickBooks has established itself as a reliable partner for SMEs looking to improve their financial operations and spur expansion.

To sum up, prosperous fintech platforms catering to small and medium-sized businesses are essential for enabling them to prosper in the current digital landscape. These platforms allow small and medium-sized enterprises

(SMEs) to surmount conventional growth constraints and enhance their competitiveness in international marketplaces by facilitating access to financing, optimizing operations, and delivering inventive tools and services. Fintech can open up new growth and opportunity channels for SMEs as it develops and spreads, propelling prosperity and economic growth for years.

CHAPTER XVI

Fintech and the Gig Economy

The relationship between Fintech and the gig economy

Fintech and the gig economy have a symbiotic relationship in which each significantly contributes to and drives the growth of the other. The short-term and freelance work arrangements that define the gig economy have increased in recent years due to changes in workforce choices and technology improvements. On the other hand, Fintech has become a significant player in the gig economy, offering the financial tools and digital infrastructure required to support the dynamic and flexible nature of gig labor.

Digital payment solutions are one of the main ways Fintech helps the gig economy. Fintech businesses have created many digital payment platforms and mobile wallets that allow gig workers to receive money swiftly and securely by avoiding the hold-ups and complications of conventional banking systems. Using these platforms, gig workers may better manage their financial flow, see their earnings in real-time, and avoid the hassles of using traditional payment methods. Fintech solutions also give gig workers more economic freedom and control, making it easier to keep track of their earnings, save money, and handle spending.

Fintech platforms are also transforming gig workers' access to financial services, as they frequently have particular financial issues and needs. Gig workers, who could have erratic revenue streams and scant documentation to support their economic activities, have long been underserved by traditional banks and financial institutions. Fintech businesses are creating cutting-edge banking and financing solutions specifically suited to the demands of gig workers by utilizing technology and other data sources. For instance, gig workers can obtain banking services like loans, debit cards, and savings accounts through digital banking systems, eliminating the need for a physical branch and a ton of paperwork. Fintech lenders can also offer loans to gig workers based not on traditional credit scores but on their potential for future earnings since they employ machine learning algorithms and data analytics to analyze credit risk more precisely and quickly.

Furthermore, for gig workers—who frequently do not have access to traditional job benefits like health insurance, disability insurance, and retirement savings plans—fintech platforms are spurring innovation in insurance and risk management. Fintech companies are creating on-demand insurance solutions targeted to gig workers' unique work arrangements and income levels. These products offer flexible coverage options. Fintech firms are also utilizing blockchain technology to establish peer-to-peer insurance networks and decentralized insurance pools, allowing gig workers to pool resources and share risks. These cutting-edge insurance options lessen the dangers of erratic income and ambiguous work circumstances, giving gig workers more financial stability and peace of mind.

In summary, Fintech and the gig economy have a mutually advantageous connection in which Fintech promotes and fosters the expansion of the gig economy and vice versa. Fintech solutions enable gig workers to access payments, banking services, and insurance products that are customized to their needs. They also give gig workers the digital infrastructure and financial tools they need to survive today's dynamic and flexible work environment. Additionally, the gig economy offers fintech companies access to a sizable and expanding pool of gig workers looking for creative ways to supplement their income. Fintech can provide new possibilities, promote financial inclusion, and empower gig workers globally as it develops and broadens its influence.

Financial services tailored for gig workers

As the financial landscape changes, financial services designed for gig workers have become increasingly important, meeting these individuals' particular demands and difficulties. Recent technological breakthroughs, shifting labor preferences, and economic upheavals have all contributed to the gig economy's explosive expansion, typified by flexible and temporary work arrangements. The necessity for financial services that are tailored to the unique needs and circumstances of gig workers is becoming increasingly apparent as they make up a sizable portion of the workforce.

Digital payment solutions are a vital financial service specifically designed for independent contractors. Because they frequently have various sources of income and variable payment schedules, gig workers may have payment needs that traditional banking systems cannot provide in real time. Gig workers may now get payments swiftly and securely without dealing with the hassles and delays of conventional banking systems, thanks to the development of digital payment platforms and mobile wallets by fintech companies. These systems give gig workers more flexibility and control over their income, enabling them to manage cash flow efficiently, access funds instantly, and simplify their financial operations.

Fintech companies also give gig workers access to financial services tailored to their requirements and preferences. Conventional banks may only sometimes be the best option for gig workers with erratic income streams and unpredictable work schedules due to their strict qualifying standards and constrained product offerings. By providing digital banking solutions specifically designed to meet the demands of gig workers, fintech and neo banking institutions are upending this market. These digital banks offer fee-free accounts, fast account setup, flexible overdraft choices, budgeting tools, and online and mobile app accessibility to gig workers. Fintech companies enable gig workers to handle their finances more efficiently and attain better financial stability by offering them banking services that are both convenient and reasonably priced.

In addition, fintech firms are advancing lending and credit for independent contractors, who could find it challenging to obtain conventional credit because of their irregular income and sparse credit history. Using technology and alternative data sources, fintech lenders are creating creative loan solutions that meet the demands of independent contractors. Gig workers' future earning potential is considered by some fintech lenders when granting short-term loans and credit lines, as opposed to traditional credit scores. Peer-to-peer lending systems also facilitate gig workers' access to fast and transparent money by allowing them to borrow from private investors prepared to fund their loans. By allowing them to invest in their companies, pay for unforeseen costs, and close revenue gaps, these fintech lending options help gig workers prosper in the gig economy.

Fintech companies are also taking care of gig workers' insurance and risk management needs, which are sometimes disregarded or underpaid by traditional insurance providers. Because they frequently do not have access to standard job benefits like health insurance, disability insurance, and retirement savings plans, gig workers are more susceptible to unforeseen financial hazards. Fintech businesses are creating flexible coverage options and on-demand insurance products to meet the demands of gig workers, providing insurance against diseases, accidents, and other unanticipated catastrophes.

In summary, providing financial services designed explicitly for gig workers is essential to the economic security and general well-being of those involved in the gig economy. Fintech companies are enabling gig workers to more skillfully manage the risks and uncertainties of gig labor by giving them access to digital payment systems, banking services, financing choices, and customized insurance products to meet their needs. Fintech businesses have an increasing chance to innovate and provide new solutions that meet the changing demands of gig workers and help them prosper in today's fast-paced, flexible work environment as the gig economy grows and changes.

Examples of Fintech platforms supporting the gig economy

Fintech platforms that facilitate the gig economy are widely available and demonstrate how technology transforms financial services to suit better the demands of those who engage in flexible and temporary work arrangements. These platforms give gig workers access to various financial services and tools, enabling them to take advantage of credit and insurance, manage their money more skillfully, and follow their entrepreneurial goals. Several noteworthy instances demonstrate how fintech is propelling and facilitating the expansion of the gig economy.

Stripe, a fintech company that offers infrastructure and payment processing solutions to online businesses, including gig economy platforms, is one well-known example. With the help of Stripe's range of goods and services, gig economy platforms can easily and securely take payments from clients, enabling transactions between consumers and sellers on websites like Airbnb, Uber, and Lyft. Stripe helps gig economy platforms concentrate on expanding their businesses and offering value to their users, rather than worrying about the intricacies of payment processing and compliance, by giving them access to a dependable and scalable payment infrastructure.

PayPal is an additional instance of a worldwide fintech corporation that provides various digital payment solutions, such as online, mobile, and peer-to-peer payments. Gig workers may quickly and securely accept payments from clients and customers using PayPal's platform, regardless of their location or preferred payment method. In addition, PayPal provides several financial services designed with gig workers in mind, such as spending tracking, invoicing, and working capital access via its PayPal Working Capital program. PayPal enables gig workers to manage their finances better and expand their companies by giving them access to various financial tools and services.

Furthermore, Jack Dorsey, a co-founder of Twitter, established Square, which has grown to become a prominent finance platform that supports the gig economy. Square offers a range of goods and services catering to small businesses and freelancers, including point-of-sale systems, business management tools, and payment processing. With the help of Square's main product, the Square Reader, independent contractors may now take payments from clients using their mobile devices without needing pricey gear or laborious setup procedures. Additionally, Square provides several tools for managing businesses, such as payroll processing, inventory control, and invoicing, all accessible via its user-friendly website. Square promotes financial inclusion and empowerment among people involved in the gig economy by giving gig workers access to low-cost, user-friendly tools to manage and expand their enterprises.

Moreover, QuickBooks' parent company, Intuit, has created several fintech products specifically designed to meet the demands of small enterprises and gig workers. With the help of the mobile software QuickBooks Self-Employed, independent contractors, freelancers, and gig workers can track their income and spending, compute taxes, and create invoices while on the road. Additionally, Intuit provides gig workers with various financial tools and resources through several other products and services, such as QuickBooks Online, Mint, and TurboTax. With the help of Intuit's fintech solutions, gig workers can confidently follow their entrepreneurial aspirations and concentrate on their work by streamlining tax compliance and financial management.

In conclusion, by giving gig workers access to various financial tools and services catered to their requirements, fintech platforms play a critical role in fostering the expansion and development of the gig economy. Fintech enables gig workers in many ways, including helping them handle their finances more efficiently, get access to credit and insurance, and follow their entrepreneurial dreams. Examples include PayPal, Square, Intuit, Stripe, and Square. Fintech companies have an increasing chance to innovate and provide new solutions that cater to the changing demands of gig workers and help them flourish in today's flexible and dynamic work environment as the gig economy continues to rise.

CONCLUSION

"Fintech: Redefining Financial Services: Innovations, Challenges, and Opportunities in the Digital Era" serves as a comprehensive guide to understanding the transformative impact of financial technology on the modern financial landscape.

Throughout the book, we have explored the innovative solutions that fintech companies are developing to revolutionize banking, payments, lending, wealth management, and insurance.

We have analyzed the challenges and opportunities that arise from the rapid evolution of fintech, including regulatory hurdles, cybersecurity threats, and the need for greater financial inclusion.

Moreover, we have examined the role of fintech in driving economic growth, promoting entrepreneurship, and empowering individuals and businesses to access financial services more efficiently and affordably.

As we conclude this journey, it is clear that fintech is reshaping the way we interact with money and transforming the financial services industry in profound ways. By embracing innovation, collaboration, and inclusivity, we can harness the full potential of fintech to create a more accessible, transparent, and inclusive financial system that benefits everyone in the digital era and beyond.

"Fintech: Redefining Financial Services" provides readers with valuable insights, strategies, and perspectives to navigate the complexities and opportunities of the fintech revolution and seize the potential for a more prosperous and inclusive financial future.

Thank you for buying and reading/ listening to our book. If you found this book useful/ helpful please take a few minutes and leave a review on the platform where you purchased our book. Your feedback matters greatly to us.

www.ingramcontent.com/pod-product-compliance
Lightning Source LLC
Chambersburg PA
CBHW071956150726
47999CB00001B/453